Parish Re

A HISTORY AND GUIDE

Stuart A. Raymond

THE FAMILY HISTORY PARTNERSHIP

Published by
The Family History Partnership
PO Box 502
Bury, Lancashire BL8 9EP
Webpage: www.familyhistorypartnership.co.uk
Email: sales@thefamilyhistorypartnership.com

in association with
S.A. & M.J. Raymond
Webpage: www.stuartraymond.co.uk
Email: samjraymond@btopenworld.com

ISBNs:
Family History Partnership: 978 1 906280 17 8
S.A. & M.J. Raymond: 978 1 899668 52 6

First Published 2009

Printed and bound by
Information Press, Southfield Road, Eynsham
Oxford OX29 4JB

Contents

Cover illustration: Ringmore Church, Devon.

Abbreviations

Acknowledgements

I am grateful to Richard Ratcliffe, Brett Langston, and Jeremy Gibson, who all read and commented on preliminary drafts of this book. Jeremy drew my attention to the godparents listed in Banbury parish register, which he edited. I am also grateful to Bob Boyd, who saw this book through the press, and to Devon Record Office, who hold most of the documents illustrated here.

Introduction

Parish registers are valuable sources for family and local historians. They record the vital events of baptism, marriage, and burial. The term 'vital events' is an Americanism, but one that deserves to be adopted in the UK. The registers in which they are recorded are vital sources of evidence for tracing ancestral pedigrees. Indeed, they may be the only evidence we have for the existence of our ancestors.

Parish registers are the earliest comprehensive records of vital events in England and Wales, dating from 1538. They are still kept, despite the fact that civil registers of births, marriages and deaths have been maintained since 1837[1]. Registers have also been kept by Nonconformists, Roman Catholics, and Jews[2]. There are a variety of other sources which may yield information about vital events, such as churchwardens' accounts, funeral certificates, newspaper announcements and reports, death duty registers, undertakers' records, monumental inscriptions, inquisitions post mortem, and manorial court rolls.

The focus in this book, however, is on parish registers. Their history and background must be understood if they are to be used effectively. Researchers need to know where they can be found, what indexes are available, and, most importantly, what pitfalls to look out for. The aim here is to outline the history of parish registers, to assess the value of the evidence they provide, and to explain how to use them.

---

[1] The best introduction is currently WOOD, TOM. *British civil registration.* 2nd ed. FFHS, 2000.

[2] For these, see STEEL, D.J. *Sources for nonconformist genealogy and family history.* National index of parish registers. 2. Society of Genealogists, 2003; STEEL, D.J., & SAMUEL, E.R. *Sources for Roman Catholic and Jewish genealogy and family history.* National index of parish registers. 3. Society of Genealogists, 1974. See also RAYMOND, S.A. *Nonconformist records: a history and guide.* Family History Partnership, forthcoming.

1. *The Parish and its Records*

Most family and local history records are arranged geographically, by administrative area. Historians must first identify the area they are interested in, then locate the records covering that area. The parish is the most important administrative area that family and local historians are likely to encounter. Originally, it was an ecclesiastical area served by a church with (usually) one priest, who owed obedience to his diocesan bishop. Most medieval churches were built by local landowners to serve their own estates. Parish boundaries therefore originally coincided with estate boundaries. By the thirteenth century, most parish boundaries were fixed, and remained fixed until at least the nineteenth century. Since then, many new parishes have been carved out of old parishes, and many old parishes have been amalgamated with others.

Civil parishes, created at the end of the nineteenth century, took over some of the civil functions which parishes had hitherto performed. Sometimes the boundaries of civil parishes coincide with those of ecclesiastical parishes, sometimes not. A full set of ecclesiastical parish boundary maps is available in Cecil Humphery-Smith's *Phillimore atlas and index of parish registers* (3rd ed. 2003). The 'Vision of Britain' website **www.visionofbritain.org.uk** provides mapping information for most English parishes. 'Genuki' **www.genuki.org.uk** also sometimes has parish maps. Many maps on both these sites are based on Ordnance Survey maps.

The original function of the parish was to maintain its church and its priest. Under the Tudors, it was given a variety of civil functions. These included the poor, the roads, law and order, and a variety of other matters. Records of parochial administration survive in abundance[3]. These include churchwardens' accounts, overseers' accounts, tithe maps, deeds, waywardens' account, glebe terriers, and a wide variety of other papers. They also include parish registers. The terms 'parish records' and 'parish registers' are often used synonomously. They should not be. Doing so obscures the fact that there are many parish records which are not registers.

---

[3] They are described in TATE, W.E. *The parish chest: a study in the records of parochial administration in England*. 3rd ed. Phillimore, 1983.

Parish registers record the baptisms, marriages and burials[4] which took place within the boundaries of the parish, usually in the church or churchyard (although baptisms might take place elsewhere). Occasionally, they might mention vital events concerning parishioners which took place elsewhere. The register of Ford (Shropshire) records the baptism of:

'Anne, d. of Thomas & Mary Geste, baptized in the p'ish of Carston, & borne in the p'ishe of Alberbury'[4].

In the register of Week St. Mary (Cornwall) is the following entry:

'Roger Bastard was buried at St. Probus the 19 day of June 1617'.

---

[4] Most entries from parish registers cited here are taken either from the works listed below, p. 54, or from printed parish registers. A few are taken from the original registers.

2. *The Early History of Parish Registers*

In the mid-sixteenth century, England underwent a religious revolution: the Reformation. Under Henry VII and earlier kings, England had been vibrantly Catholic. It is still impossible to travel more than a few miles in the English countryside without seeing unmistakeable evidence of that vibrancy. That evidence often dominates the landscape. Innumerable churches of the fifteenth and early sixteenth centuries bear witness to the enthusiasm with which Englishmen of the period set out to create buildings worthy of their God.

Under Henry VIII and Edward VI, the exuberant progress of Roman Catholicism was abruptly interrupted. Henry's need for a divorce compelled him to rely on those who pressed for reform of the church - men like Thomas Cromwell, to whom he gave the unique office of vicegerent. Cromwell was given greater authority over the church than any other layman has ever exercised, before or since. His injunctions of 1536 and 1538 laid the basis for the English Reformation. Out went traditional practices such as the veneration of images and pilgrimages to saints' shrines. In came English Bibles - and the keeping of parish registers of baptisms, marriages and burials.

Registers were already being kept on the continent. Ironically, they were of Roman Catholic origin, having first been instituted by Cardinal Ximenes, Archbishop of Toledo, in 1497. Ximenes' initiative received the approbation of the Council of Trent in 1563. The Council issued a decree requiring that:

'The parish priest shall have a book in which he shall record the names of the persons united in marriage and of the witnesses and also the day on which and the place where the marriage was contracted, and this book he shall carefully preserve'.

This decree did not, of course, apply to the Church of England, but it is interesting that Catholics and Protestants were united on this issue. Researchers in Catholic countries can expect to find registers similar to those found in England.

The 1538 injunctions issued by Cromwell ordered parochial incumbents to

'kepe one boke or registere wherein ye shall write the day and yere of every weddyng christenyng and buryeng made within yor parishe for your tyme, and so every man succeedyng you lykewise. And shall there insert every persons name that shalbe so weddid christened or buried. And for the sauff kepinge of the same boke the parishe shalbe bonde to provide of these comen charges one sure coffer with twoo lockes and keys whereof the one to remayne with you, and the other with the said wardens, wherein the said boke shalbe laide upp. Whiche boke ye shall every Sonday take furthe and in the presence of the said wardens or one of them write and recorde in the same all the weddinges christenynges and buryenges made the hole weke before. And that done to lay upp the boke in the said coffer as afore. And for every tyme that the same shalbe omytted the partie that shalbe in the faulte thereof shall forfett to the saide churche iijs iiijd to be emploied on the reparation of the same church'[5].

The official reason given for keeping registers was 'to avoid dispute touching ages, titles or lineal descents'[6]. Contemporaries, however, were 'in greate feer and mystrust' [suspecting that] 'somme charges, more than hath byn in tymys past, schall grow to theym by this occaycyon off regesstrynge off thes thyngges'[7].

This had been one of the rumours which had helped to ignite the Pilgrimage of Grace[8]. If it was indeed Cromwell's plan to tax vital events, then he was thwarted by the need to avoid giving cause for further rebellion. The Pilgrimage of Grace, which had just been defeated when the injunctions were issued, was a close shave for the regime. It was too dangerous to tax baptisms, marriages and burials.

Nevertheless, registration began. The churchwardens of Ashburton (Devon) paid 3s 6d

'for a new book bought this year in which to enter everyone who dies within this parish and who receives the sacrament of baptism according to the order of the illustrious prince Henry the Eighth, King, defender of the faith, and on earth supreme head of the Church of England'[9].

Many of Cromwell's injunctions had a bumpy ride in the following reigns. They were tightened up and made more protestant under Edward VI (1547-1553). They were mostly discarded by Queen Mary

[5] COX, J.CHARLES. *The parish registers of England*. 1910, p.2-3.
[6] *Letters and papers, foreign and domestic, of the reign of Henry VIII*, vol.**13**(2). 1893, p.486.
[7] BURN, JOHN SOUTHERDEN. *The history of parish registers in England*. 1862, p.9; Cox, op cit, p.4.
[8] *Letters and papers, foreign and domestic, reign of Henry VIII*, vol.**12**(1), 1891, p.85, 164, & 460.
[9] HANHAM, ALISON, ed. *Churchwardens accounts of Ashburton, 1479-1580*. Devon & Cornwall Record Society new series **15**. 1970, p.104.

(1553-1558). They were re-imposed - this time for good - when Elizabeth I came to the throne in 1558. The order to keep parish registers, however, was enforced under all three monarchs. In 1547, this injunction was re-issued by Edward VI[10]. In 1555, and again in 1557, Cardinal Pole directed bishops to check whether registers were being kept, and ordered that the names of godparents should be recorded[11]. In 1559, Elizabeth again re-issued the injunction[12], although omitting the instruction about godparents. Rumours about taxes on baptisms and marriages forced her to issue a denial in 1560[13].

The utility of parish registers was recognised from their beginning, despite the suspicions which they engendered. Cromwell had not, however, made adequate provision either for their preservation, or for ease of access to them. Transcripts of registers to be kept in diocesan registries began to be made early in Elizabeth's reign. In 1563, and again in 1590, attempts were made to provide an adequate legislative framework for these transcripts. It was not, however, until 1597 that definitive action was taken. In that year, Convocation proposed new canons, which were approved by Queen Elizabeth in 1598. These included new instructions on the keeping of parish registers, substantially incorporated in canons issued soon after the accession of James I. The 1604 canons instructed churchwardens:

> 'once every year, within one month after the twenty-fifth of March, [to] transmit unto the bishop of the diocese, or his chancellor, a true copy of the names of all persons christened, married or buried in their parish in the year before, and the certain days and months in which every such christening, marriage and burial was had, to be subscribed with the hand of the said minister and churchwardens, to the end the same may faithfully be preserved in the registry of the said bishop; which certificate shall be received without fee'[14].

This was the origin of the keeping of bishops' transcripts (BTs). In the sixteenth century, the year normally ended on 25th March. BTs provide us with valuable checks on entries in parish registers.

The 1598 and 1604 canons also ordered that registers should henceforth be kept on parchment, for their better preservation. Hitherto, they

[10] Ibid, p.18.
[11] COX, op cit, p.4. See below, p.27.
[12] HUGHES, PAUL L., & LARKIN, JAMES F., eds. *Tudor royal proclamations volume II: the later Tudors (1553-1587)*. 1969, p.120.
[13] Ibid, p.161.
[14] BRAY, GERALD, ed. *The Anglican canons 1529-1947*. Church of England Record Society 6. 1998, p.361.

had mostly been written on paper. Every parish was to purchase a new book,

> 'wherein shall be written the day and year of every christening, wedding, burial which have been in that parish since the time that the law was first made in that behalf, so far as the ancient books thereof can be procured, but especially since the beginning of the reign of the late queen'.[15]

The wording was unfortunate. Many incumbents took it to mean that it was not necessary to transcribe entries prior to 1558. Consequently, they destroyed most of the old paper books, so that much information for the period 1538-1558 was lost.

Registers occasionally record the process of transcription. At Loughborough in 1601, for example:

> 'John Dawson did copy and write out this book out of the old paper book when he was at the age of three score and one years ...'

The task of transcribing the old registers was usually done neatly, although for the most part we cannot check accuracy. Parish registers for Elizabeth's reign are generally all in the same hand. They are often signed by the incumbent and churchwardens in office when the transcript was made. Their signatures were intended to authenticate that transcription, in accordance with the new canons. That transcription may not have been made until well into the seventeenth century. The researcher should be wary of treating these signatures as having been written at the time when the vital events recorded actually took place. A sixteenth-century register that has identical signatures in it for every year from 1538 to 1598 provides no proof of the longevity of incumbents and churchwardens.

For the future, the canon of 1604 ordered that

> 'upon every sabbath day, immediately after morning or evening prayer, the minister and churchwardens shall take the said parchment book out of the said coffer, and the minister, in the presence of the churchwardens, shall write and record in the said book the names of all persons christened, together with the names and surnames of their parents, and also the names of all persons married and buried in that parish in the week before, and the day and year of every such christening marriage and burial, and that done, they shall lay up that book in the coffer ... and the minister and churchwardens unto every page of that book, when it shall be filled with such inscriptions, shall subscribe their names'.

---

[15]   Ibid, p. 361.

Parish registers and bishops' transcripts continued to be kept throughout the reigns of the first two Stuart monarchs. However, when the rule of Charles I degenerated into civil war, register keeping suffered. Many registers between 1642 and 1653 were badly kept, or not kept at all. In the register of North Lydbury (Shropshire) is noted against the years from 1643 to 1647 'these years being time of war the Register was neglected'.

Parliament was concerned about this neglect. When its presbyterian *Directory* was substituted for the *Prayer Book* in 1645, it was ordered that each parish should keep

'a fair register book of velim'[16].

This was to note not only the dates of baptism and burial, but also the dates of birth and death. The names of the parents of children baptised were also to be recorded. Few surviving registers from the period include all these details.

A more revolutionary reform was attempted by the Barebones Parliament in 1653[17]. Marriage became a civil matter, without the participation of clergy. Justices of the Peace were to perform the ceremony. If desired, the couple could obtain a certificate of marriage from the officiating JP. The certificate could then be presented to the Clerk of the Peace, who was required to record it in a register maintained for the purpose, and kept with other Quarter Sessions records. This was presumably intended as a replacement for bishops' transcripts. Such registers are not known to have survived.

The principal marriage record continued to be the parish register, kept by an official called the 'parish register'. He was to be elected by the ratepayers in each parish, subject to the approval of a JP. He was to hold office for three years. Sometimes, but not always, incumbents or parish clerks were chosen to fill the office. The parish register's duty was to register not only marriages, but also births (not baptisms) and deaths. He could charge a fee of 12d per marriage, and 4d per birth or death. The election of officers was sometimes recorded in parish registers. This example occurs in a Northamptonshire register:

'Thomas Barber of Long Buckby ... was according to the Act of Parlment in that case made Elected and Chosen by the maior parte of the inhabitants to be Parish Register, who according to directions of the said hath taken his corporate Oath befour me for his true p[er]forming the said office this 9th of Nouember 1653. [signed] Edward Farmer'.

The act of 1653 also required the 'register' to call the banns of marriage on three successive 'Lord's Days', 'in the public meeting place called the

---

[16] FIRTH, C.H., & RAIT, R.S., eds. *Acts and ordinances of the interregnum, 1642-1660*. H.M.S.O., 1910, vol.2, p.715-8.   [17] Ibid, p.715-8.

church or chapel', or, alternatively, in the adjoining market-place on three successive market days. Such banns were sometimes entered in the parish register.

Interregnum registers, where they survive, were generally well kept. Frequently, however, they do not survive. It is probable that many registers were not handed over to the Restoration clergy by the lay 'parish registers'. And it may be that some clergy did not regard them as valid. The attitude of the restored clergy towards those who had displaced them is well summarised in the Courteenhall (Northamptonshire) register. Between 1645 and 1650, William Ponder signed the register as 'rector'. The word has been repeatedly crossed out and the word 'intruder' substituted.

The act of 1653 did not remain in force for very long. When Charles II was restored to the throne in 1660, acts of the Interregnum 'Parliaments' were regarded as illegal. A special act had to be passed to legalise marriages which had been conducted by JPs. The Restoration restored the task of keeping parish registers to the clergy. Many registers record a

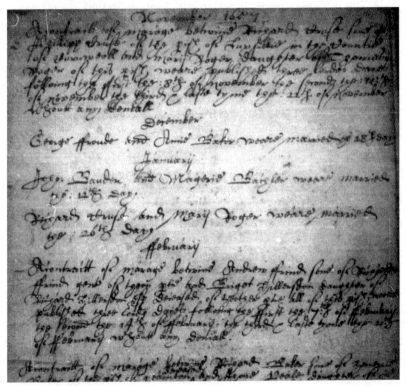

Figure 1. Marriage entries from the Interregnum register of Holbeton, Devon. Note the records of banns being called. Devon Record Office Holbeton MF2.

large number of baptisms at this time. They do not record a post-restoration baby boom. Rather, these entries reflect the fact that many babies had not been baptised during the Interregnum. The restoration clergy saw to it that the unbaptised young people of their parishes received a belated baptism; many must have been five or ten years old in 1660. Indeed, a new office 'for the ministration of baptism to such as are of riper years' had to be approved by Convocation in 1661. Family historians should not assume that baptismal entries from the restoration period provide proofs of age.

After the Restoration, as nonconformity became more prevalent, so the need to baptise nonconformists who turned to the Church of England increased. Neither the Baptists, nor members of the Society of Friends (Quakers) practised infant baptism. The fact that some of the newly baptised were adults is not necessarily apparent in registers.

There was little change in the way parish registers were kept in the ensuing century. Acts ordering burial in woollen were passed in 1666 and 1678. This is frequently mentioned in burial entries. In 1694, the fears that had been voiced by Tudor rebels became reality, and a tax was imposed on births, marriages and deaths. Collection was based on the information provided by parish registers. Incumbents were instructed to expand the coverage of registers by recording *all* births, not just Church of England baptisms. The instruction was rarely obeyed, although there are occasional exceptions to this rule. The register of Atworth (Wiltshire), for example, lists the births of 'Annabaptistes and Quakers' between 1697 and 1704. The register of Moulton (Northamptonshire) has a 'list of unbaptized children and excommunicated persons' compiled between 1693 and 1721.

An act of indemnity was passed in 1706 to indemnify the numerous clergy who had failed to collect the tax. There was undoubtedly some under-registration of vital events as a result of the 1694 legislation, but the tax was abolished in 1705. Few assessments made under this act survive. However, assessments for London and Bristol have been published, and provide valuable listings of the inhabitants of these cities[18].

---

[18] GLASS, D.V., ed. *London inhabitants within the walls 1695*. London Record Society **2**. 1966; RALPH, ELIZABETH, & WILLIAMS, MARY E., eds. *The inhabitants of Bristol in 1696*. Bristol Record Society publication **25**. 1968.

3. *Marriage Laws & Customs*

The early history of parish registers outlined above has to be seen against the background of marriage laws and customs. It has frequently been assumed that a church wedding was always the norm before the nineteenth century. That assumption is not correct. Marriage in England was not originally an ecclesiastical matter. Valid marriages, under the common law, simply required the consent of the parties to an agreement made before witnesses. In the medieval period, it gradually became the custom to obtain the blessing of the church upon such betrothals. Betrothal still took place, before witnesses, but it was followed by a ceremony at the church door. Nevertheless, betrothal without a church ceremony continued to be popularly regarded as marriage, and as entitling the partners to behave as man and wife. By the sixteenth century, the vast majority of marriage ceremonies were conducted in church. It was reasonable for Cromwell to assume that the keeping of parish registers would result in all marriages being recorded. Ecclesiastical law developed at a faster rate than the common law.

The church insisted that a marriage could only be valid if it was preceded either by the calling of banns, or the grant of a licence. A licence was only supposed to be granted for marriage in the home parish of one of the parties. The common law, however, took precedence over ecclesiastical law. Bishops could prosecute priests within their jurisdictions who ignored the need for banns or licences. But they could not invalidate the marriages they conducted, nor could they exercise any control over priests operating in liberties or peculiars outside their jurisdiction.

There were many such liberties and peculiars, especially in London. In the late seventeenth century, the ecclesiastical authorities fought running battles trying to prevent irregular marriages at places such as Holy Trinity, Minories, St. James's, Duke's Place, and St. Botolph's, Aldgate. There were no less than 1,803 marriages at Duke's Place in 1690 alone[19]. This represented a substantial loss of income for the clergy who should have conducted those marriages. Legislation in 1695 stamped out most of this trade in ecclesiastical peculiars. It failed, however, to tackle the root of the problem. It did not invalidate common law marriages. It did not stamp out irregular marriages in places where bishops had no jurisdic-

---

[19] BENTON, TONY. *Irregular marriages in London before 1754.* 2nd ed. Society of Genealogists, 2000, p.20.

tion, such as the Fleet Prison. The Fleet was a royal peculiar, outside the Bishop of London's jurisdiction. It was a debtors' prison. In the early eighteenth century, many of the priests who conducted services there were themselves imprisoned debtors. They had nothing to lose from episcopal censure. By the middle of the century, perhaps half of all London's marriages were being conducted irregularly in the Fleet. The celebrants of Fleet marriages kept their own registers, many of which are now in the National Archives. Some have recently been published[20].

The development of other marriage centres was helped by the fact that the grantors of marriage licences increasingly ignored the canonical requirement that marriage should take place in the home parish of one of the parties. Between 1692 and 1754, there were 2,655 marriages at St. Mary Magdalene, Oxford, most of them for non-parishioners. The Bishop of Oxford's Registry, where licences were granted, was at the back of the church[21]. A number of similar marriage centres grew up in other parts of the country, for example, at St.Nicholas's church in Rochester (Kent), Fledborough (Nottinghamshire), and Peak Forest (Derbyshire).

---

[20] HERBER, MARK, ed. *Clandestine marriages in the Chapel and Rules of the Fleet Prison, 1680-1754*. 3 vols to date. Francis Boutle Publishers, 1998-2001.

[21] BENTON, op cit, p.42.

4. *Lord Hardwicke's Marriage Act, 1753*

In 1753, just a century after the Barebones Act of 1653, Parliament took decisive action to end the scandal of irregular and clandestine marriages, which not only deprived clergy of their legitimate income, but also nullified parental authority, and threatened the descent of property. The act ended the practice of common law marriage. It invalidated all marriages not preceded by the calling of banns or the grant of a licence. Betrothals ceased to be regarded as lawful marriage. All marriages, except those of Jews and Quakers, had to be conducted by an Anglican clergyman in the home parish of one of the two parties. Minors had to have the consent of their parents or guardians. Marriage of boys under the age of 14 was prohibited, as was marriage of girls under 12.

The act also had an important impact on the way in which marriages were registered. For the first time, they had to be recorded in a prescribed format. Printed forms began to be used. Both parties had to sign the register, as did witnesses. Banns also had to be recorded in a printed book. The use of printed forms meant that marriage registers were kept much more carefully after 1753.

The act did have unexpected consequences. Its drafters specified that marriage could only take place in churches where banns had hitherto usually been published. That prevented marriages taking place in churches such as St. Paul's Cathedral and Westminster Abbey, as banns had never been called in them. It also prevented marriages taking place in newly-built churches.

5. Parish Registers after 1753

Another attempt to impose a duty on parish register entries was made by the Stamp Act of 1783. Three pence per entry was to be paid. The incumbent of Hawstead All Saints (Suffolk) thought it

'a tax most vexatious to the clergy, and which, it is thought, will be unproductive to the state'.

The Sturminster Marshall (Dorset) register notes:

'account carried in to Governmt to the 1st of August 1788'

This duty, like that of 1694, may again have discouraged parents from having their babies baptised. Paupers were exempt. In some registers the letter 'P' against an entry denotes pauper. At Glasbury, Breconshire, seven of the nineteen burials in 1785 were marked 'EP', that is, 'exempt, pauper'.

The number of people declaring themselves to be paupers naturally rose. The act was repealed in 1794[22]. On occasion, a baptism after 1794 may be of a child whose parents delayed baptism because they were unwilling to pay the duty. There are no surviving records of assessments other than the parish registers themselves.

The format of entries was standardised by the acts of 1753 and 1812. However, in the parish register of Selby (Yorkshire) we read:

'The remainder of the Baptisms & Burials in the year 1777 are inserted in a New Register according to the form required by the Archbishop, in the Articles for his Primary Visitation'.

Archbishop Markham was adopting a mode of entry pioneered by Wiliam Dade, a York clergyman. Dade registers, as they are known, are found primarily in the dioceses of York and Chester[23]. Dade registers are not alone. Bishop Barrington introduced a similar format in the Diocese of Durham in 1796.

The use of printed forms for marriage registers after 1753 was obviously successful – so much so that in 1812 Rose's Act decreed that,

---

[22] Death duties were instituted in 1795. It is not clear whether there was a connection.

[23] Bellingham, Roger. 'The Dade parish registers', *Family history news and digest* **10**(2), 1995, p.76-9; BELLINGHAM, ROGER. 'Dade registers', *Archives* **27**(107), 2002, p.134-47; BELLINGHAM, ROGER. 'Dade parish registers' *Local population studies*, **73**, 2004, p.51-60.

with effect from 1st January 1813, printed forms should also be used for baptism and burial entries. Ministers were to sign each entry. This act ended the use of parchment books, although bishops' transcripts still had to be written on parchment. The King's Printer provided new registers printed in the required format; they included a copy of the Act. These registers are much easier to use, although the miscellaneous notes which had hitherto been made in registers mostly ceased.

By the early nineteenth century, the parochial registration system was no longer considered to be fit for its purpose. Under-registration was endemic. Industrialisation and the migration of industrial workers reduced the number of babies brought for baptism. Nonconformists - if they accepted infant baptism - increasingly used their own baptismal rites. But their registers were not accepted as legal evidence.

It was not, however, the nonconformist complaints which led to the introduction of civil registration. Rather, it was the need for adequate proof of title in a society where inheritance determined the ownership of land[24]. That need could not, however, override the vested interest of the church in maintaining parish registers. From 1837, two systems of registration ran in parallel. The General Register Office and its civil registers served the needs of the propertied. The Office has been described as 'the centre of a system for recording property rights'[25]. Parish registers continued to serve the needs of the church, and, indeed, are still kept today.

Since 1st July 1837, parish marriage registers have been duplicates of the civil registers. The parish copy, unless it is still in use, is likely to have been deposited in a record office, where it can easily be consulted. The Registrar's copy can only be consulted by purchasing individual certificates, which must be identified by using indexes which (at the time of writing) are sometimes of dubious quality.

Civil registration had no immediate impact on the keeping of parochial baptism and burial registers. Baptismal and burial entries in the latter may sometimes be more informative than birth and death entries in the civil registers. However, the decline in church attendance, and the increasing use of non-parochial cemeteries, mean that the proportion of vital events recorded in parish registers has decreased substantially in the last 150 years or so.

Not all vital events presided over by Anglican clergymen took place in parish churches. They could also be registered in the chapels of institutions such as hospitals, cathedrals, schools and colleges, workhouses,

[24] HIGGS, EDWARD. *Life, death and statistics: civil registration, censuses and the work of the General Register Office, 1836-1952*. Local Population Studies, 2004, chapter 1, provides a detailed discussion of the origins of civil registration.
[25] Higgs, op cit, p.216.

and prisons. Cemeteries also kept their own registers, as did overseas churches, forces chaplains, and diplomatic missions. The term 'non-parochial registers' is often used to refer to nonconformist registers. It should more properly be reserved for the registers of institutions such as these.

6. *The Content of Parish Registers*

The earliest registers were kept in paper books. In a small number of parishes, entries pre-date 1538[26]. It is probable that such entries were copied in 1538 from pre-existing sources which had been compiled for other purposes. Vital events were often recorded in church psalters and missals. Proofs of age given in inquisitions post mortem frequently mention them. When John Adekyn of Newton, Norfolk, was baptised, a number of witnesses saw the priest 'write the date in a missal in their presence ... and so they know the date'[27]. John Smyter and Edward Bayer, when testifying to the age of William Bonevyle in 1414, reported that they were present at his baptism, and that 'the date was written in English in a book and read out whilst they were there'. The chaplain who baptised the baby wrote the entry[28].

It is probable that many entries from missals, psalters, and perhaps bede rolls[29], were copied into parish registers in 1538. If so, unfortunately, most have been lost. They were not copied when the old paper registers were transcribed into parchment registers in accordance with the canons of 1598 and 1604.

Surviving sixteenth-century registers are almost all transcripts made after 1598. Entries made before 1558 were frequently not transcribed. Furthermore, many entries post-1558 were probably abbreviated, and omit information that was in the original registers.

Steel[30] points out that many later registers are also copies which were not written at the time of the events they record. The fact that the canons required registers to be written up every Sunday was ignored in practice. Instead, details of events were frequently scribbled into a rough memoranda book, or even on to scraps of paper, from which the register could

---

[26] Cox, op cit, p.239, identified 18 registers that may pre-date 1538.

[27] *Calendar of inquisitions post mortem ... vol. XIX, 7-14 Henry IV (1405-1413)*, 1992, p.278.

[28] *Calendar of inquisitions post mortem ... vol.XX. 1-5 Henry V (1413-1418)*. 1995, p.45.

[29] Bede rolls were lists of people who had left bequests to the church, in anticipation that their souls would benefit from prayers.

[30] STEEL, D.J. *National index of parish registers. Volume 1. Sources of births, marriages and deaths before 1837 (1)*. Society of Genealogists, 1968, p.27-31.

be written up later. In some cases, it is evident that the registers were only written up once a year, perhaps at the same time as bishops' transcripts were prepared, or immediately prior to the Archdeacon's visitation. It is even possible that they were copied from the bishops' transcripts; that would explain why, on occasion, the latter contain more information than registers. The keeping of rough notes from which registers could be written up later was specifically forbidden by Rose's Act, 1812. The practice was evidently still common in the early nineteenth century. Many scribes continued the practice after 1812, despite the Act.

Until 1753, there was no set format in which parish register entries had to be made. All that the canons required was that the incumbent and the churchwardens should sign the registers at the end of each year's entries. The lack of a set format meant that the mode of keeping a register depended on the whim, or the eccentricities, of the scribe. The latter was not necessarily the incumbent. Parish clerks frequently took on the duty. Some parishes employed a scrivenor to write up the register at the end of every year.

Professional scrivenors, hopefully, had good handwriting. Nevertheless, it still may not be easy to read. Sixteenth and seventeenth century handwriting differs from modern handwriting, and reading it requires practice. There are many texts to help the beginner[31]. There is also a web-based tutorial at 'Palaeography: reading old handwriting' **www.nationalarchives.gov.uk/palaeography**.

Spelling may also be problematical. The way in which names were spelt was not fixed, and the same name may be spelt in a variety of different ways, e.g. Raymond, Reymond, Raymont. The persons concerned were often illiterate themselves, and the scribe sometimes only semi-literate. Names were often written phonetically, and spelling may have been affected by local dialect.

A greater problem lies in the fact that early registers were frequently written in Latin. The terms 'baptizatus erat', 'nupti erat', and 'sepultus erat' became common form, although the use of the language was questioned at an early date. Richard Kilbie, minister of All Saints, Derby in 1610, wrote in his register that he could

'see no reason why a register for English people should be written in Latin'.

On the other hand, in the register of Bebington (Cheshire), Latin replaced English from 1584. The earliest entry reads:

'1558 Nov' The 18th day was buried Cicelye Williamson'.

However, from 'mensis August', 1584, Latin was used:

'Emota filia Johnis Scarbrick de Beb. bap 22ᴺ'

---

[31] For example, MUNBY, LIONEL. *Reading Tudor and Stuart handwriting*. Phillimore, 1988.

During the Interregnum the use of Latin was abandoned, although it made a brief re-appearance after 1660. It totally disappeared after 25th March, 1733 when its use in courts of law was abolished.

The alteration of the calendar in 1751 obviously affected the keeping of parish registers, but most scribes were content to make no comment when 11 days were 'lost' in September 1751, or when they began the year 1752 on 1st January instead of 25th March, as hitherto. Occasionally, more notice was taken. At Moulton (Northamptonshire) the words 'new style' were added after the year for every year until 1755, as if the scribe expected to have to revert to 'old style' at some future date. At Glasbury (Breconshire) a new volume of the register was begun on 1st January 1752. Sometimes a more detailed explanation of the change is given.

In other cases, the new style was used at a much earlier date. In the Banbury (Oxfordshire) register, the year began on 1st January as early as 1558.

Parish register entries were usually made consecutively, although sometimes baptisms and burials were separated from marriages, in some cases being made in a separate book. The way in which entries were made may, on occasion, provide evidence that the registers were not written up immediately after the events they recorded. If all the baptisms for a year are immediately followed by all the marriages, and then by all the burials, the likelihood is that the register was written up annually. This may also be the cause of entries being written out of sequence.

The amount of detail recorded in each entry prior to the acts of 1753 and 1812 varies considerably. Sixteenth-century registers were frequently abbreviated when they were transcribed in accordance with the canons of 1598 and 1604[32]. The labour of transcribing had to be paid for, and abbreviation offered a way of reducing costs. Consequently, sixteenth-century registers may provide limited detail. Later entries sometimes record information such as relationships, occupations, addresses, and ages. There are, for example, many entries for the baptisms and burials of nurse children in and around London. Paupers are identified in many registers. The tribulations of the poor are graphicaly described in this entry from the Staplehurst (Kent) register:

'1578. There was comytted to the earth the body of Johan Longley, who died in the highway as she was carryed on horseback to have been conveyed from officer to officer, tyll she should have come to the parish of Hayershe'.

On occasion a scribe recorded his opinion of the people whose vital events he recorded. Mr James Haines of Titchbury, buried in Hartland, Devon, in 1758,

'was an honest worthy neighbour and a good parishioner'.

---

[32] Cox, op cit, p.17.

Such opinions can sometimes be rather more colourful. An entry from Buxted (Sussex) for 1666 reads:

'Richard Bassett the old clarke of this parish ... whose melody warbled forth as if he had been thumped on the back with a stone, was buried 20 Sept'.

At Breadsall (Derbyshire) in 1773 took place the burial of:

'Mr.Joseph Jackson (a miser under a heap of riches)'

The scribe at Shillingstone (Dorset) did not mince his words when, in 1742, he recorded:

'David Pitman and Mary Haskell, a rogue and a whore, married'

Parish registers were also receptacles for miscellaneous notes, orders, accounts, etc., relating to parish business. The Week St. Mary register, for example, includes an order from Cornwall Quarter Sessions relating to vagabonds. At Eastwell (Kent), the register records a number of loyalty oaths taken during the civil war: the Protestation, the Solemn League and Covenant, and the Vow and Covenant – all with the signatures of adult males. The register of Bushley, Worcestershire, has notes regarding two legacies left to the parish in 1708-9, records 'there was the highest flood that ever was known' in 1770, and has a list of collections for briefs (i.e.charitable collections authorised by the Crown) made between 1670 and 1692. Notes on briefs are frequently found: in 1678, for example, the people of Crowhurst (Sussex) raised 28s 8d towards the rebuilding of St. Pauls Cathedral – and the rector listed the names of contributors in the parish register.

The interpretation of entries in parish registers is not always straightforward. It is easy to confuse different families who have similar surnames. In some families, children were given the same christian names as siblings who had died. The terms 'the elder' and 'the younger' may be applied to fathers and sons, or to brothers with the same name. The 'younger' may in course of time become the 'elder' when he in turn has a son of the same name. The entry for a burial may use a different form of the name than was used in baptismal or marriage entries, e.g. 'Harry' for Henry, 'Dick' for Richard. Where ages are given, they are not necessarily reliable.

The *raison d'etre* of parish registers was to record baptisms, marriages and burials. It is important to appreciate that not all vital events were recorded. Puritanism in the Elizabethan era, followed by the rise of nonconformist denominations after the Restoration, reduced the number of Church of England baptisms that took place. Baptismal entries were less likely to be made in parish registers than entries for marriages or burials. Married couples needed to be able to prove that they had been married, and so tended to make sure that a register entry was made. Even non-conformists insisted on their right to be buried in the parish churchyard. Belief in infant baptism, however, was not shared by all. Baptists and Quakers did not have their babies baptised. Congregationalists and Presbyterians often baptised them themselves. Such baptisms were not normally recorded in parish registers, unless the government wanted to tax them.

Baptism - the ritual washing away of sins - is the rite by which new members are welcomed into membership of the church. The unbaptised could not enter heaven, and child mortality was heavy, so babies were usually baptised within a few days of birth. The 1662 *Book of common prayer* instructed the clergy to 'admonish the people that they defer not the baptisms of their children longer than the first or second Sunday next after their birth'. In an emergency, baptism could be carried out privately by the midwife or other lay person. These baptisms are sometimes referred to as 'half-baptisms'. Such baptisms should have been registered, but many probably were not. Rose's Act 1812 insisted that they should be. The baby, if it survived, should have been brought into church to be 'received'. An entry in the register of St. Mary's, Lichfield for 1591 records that

> 'Margarett Dr. of Walter Henningham de Pypehall, baptized by the mydwyfe, and as yett not brought to ye churche to be there examyned and testified by them that were present'.

By contrast, at Clyst St.George (Devon) is recorded:

> 'Eliza, Daughter of William & Elizabeth Goldsworthy (received into church after private baptism on 6th June) June 19 1810'

The second ceremony was sometimes referred to as a 'christening', although the term could also be applied to the actual ceremony of baptism. Midwives, incidentally, had to be licenced by the bishop to ensure that they were sufficiently trustworthy to carry out baptisms. Records of their licences can often be found in diocesan records[33]. One of the articles in Cardinal Pole's Canterbury Diocese visitation of 1557 asked

> 'whether they [the clergy] be diligent in teaching the midwives how to christen children in time of necessity according to the Canons of the Church, or no?'[34].

---

[33] For more information, see GRUNDY, JOAN E. *History's midwives, including a C17th and C18th Yorkshire midwives nominations index*. FFHS, 2003.

[34] FRERE, WALTER HOWARD, ed. *Visitation articles and injunctions of the period of the Reformation. Volume II. 1536-1558*. Alcuin Club collections **15**. 1910, p.422.

Private baptism should not have been carried out
'without ... great cause and necessity',

according to the prayer book. It was, however, often abused in the eighteenth and nineteenth centuries. Nonconformists sometimes used the
ceremony as a means of having their children's names recorded in the
register, without bringing them into church. Some of the 'better sort' felt
that public baptism for their children was an invasion of privacy. They
were able to insist on private baptism. Indeed, a few London churches
have separate registers of private baptisms[35]. In other registers, entries
such as this from Worcester Cathedral can be found:

'1804, July 30. Elizabeth Laetitita, d. of the Rev. John Wingfield (a
prebendary of this Cathedral) & Mary his wife, was b.July 26 and privately baptized'.

The generally short interval between birth and baptism means that
baptismal registers can be used as a surrogate for birth registers from the
sixteenth to the nineteenth centuries[36]. Mostly, they recorded at least the
name of the child and his father. Sometimes mothers' names were also
given, and other information might be added. If the child was illegitimate, details might sometimes be given, as in this entry from the register
of Churchill in Oswaldslow, Worcestershire:

'Margarett A bastard child begotten by Richard Clarke on ye body of
Alice Price wid: was babtized ye 10th day of March 1681/2'.

The epithets 'whore' or 'harlot' might be added to the mother's name.
In 1604, the Week St. Mary (Cornwall) register records the baptism of:

'Susannah the bastard of Zenobia Mayne, harlot'

A very few churches kept separate registers for bastard baptisms[37]. There
are often many entries for illegitimate baptisms in the registers of churches
which had workhouses in their parish, such as St. Matthew's, Exeter.

In the baptism of infants, promises were made on behalf of the child
by godparents. Baptismal entries which name godparents are surprisingly infrequent, except during the reign of Queen Mary. It was important for Roman Catholics to record the names of godparents, in order to
avoid the crime of 'spiritual incest'. It was forbidden, for example, to
marry your mother's god-child, as she would be your spiritual sister.

---

[35] STEEL, op cit, p.46.
[36] This is discussed in detail by WRIGLEY, E.A., & SCHOFIELD, R.S. *The
population history of England 1541-1871.* Edward Arnold, 1981, p.96-7.
Adult baptisms were rare, although their numbers increased in the
18th century.
[37] STEEL, op cit, p.49.

BANBURY PARISH REGISTER

VOLUME ONE   1558 - 1653   BAPTISMS
Anno Dni. 1558

This booke entreth the first day of Januarie in the first yeere
of the Raigne of our Soveraigne Ladie Queene Elizabeth which
representeth all the childrens names baptized, and the names
of such as have been Maried, and of such as have been Buried
within the Prebendarie of Banbury.

1558

Herein are conteyned the names of all such persons, with the day and
yeere, as were baptized, married and buried from the first yeere of the rayne
of our Soveraigne Ladie Elizabeth by the grace of God Queen of England France
and Ireland defender of the faith, etc.   And in the yeere of our Lorde God 1558
within the Prebendarie of Banburie.

				Godparents
Jan	24	BULL	Henrie	Henrie Greene
				John Goodriche, Alice Horneslye
Feb	1	BROWNE	George s of Thomas	Henry Shuttlewoorth
				Thomas Danvers, Alice Horneslye
	4	SHORTE	Friswide d of Robert	John Warner
				Friswide Barnesley, Jane Knight
	16	TEY	Annys d of John	John Traforde
				Alice Halhed, Marie Goodrich
	16	PYNER	Alice d of George	William Copland
				Alice West, Elizabeth Knight
	20	WALSOLL	William	William Weston
				John Redshawe, Alice Hornesley
	26	KNIGHT	Elizabeth	William Short
				Elizabeth Goodrich, Alice Hornesley
Mar	3	HUYCK	Alice	Thomas Allen
				Alice Huyck, Elizabeth Roberts
	8	DARBY	Fryswyde	John Knight
				Friswide Barnesley, Elizabeth Knight
	9	DRIVER	Alice	Roger Jackson
				Elionour Wilsheire, Alice Mortymer
	19	SOWTHAM	Annys	Thomas Sowtham
				Annys Long, Annys Bull
	27	PEDLEY	Thomas	Nycholas Puddle
				Thomas Allen, Margaret Shorte
	25	SHERWOOD	Annys	Roberte Sowtham
				Annys Sowtham, Margaret Richardes
	25	SHERWOOD	Annys	John Huyck
				Annys Bull, Isabell Baylie
Apr	7	WISDOME	Friswide	Richard West
				Friswide Barnesley, Elizabeth Goodrych
	7	HEYTON	Alice	Thomas Symons
				Alice Hornesley, Joane Basse
	10	HAWTEN	Jane	Richarde Moore
				Jane Cooke, Annys Foeye [?]

Figure 2. A page from Gibson, J.S.W., ed. *Baptism and burial registers of Banbury, Oxfordshire.* Banbury Historical Society 7. 1965. Note that godparents are listed in accordance with Cardinal Pole's injunctions of 1555 and 1557.

Such reasoning lay behind Cardinal Ximenes introduction of parish registers into Spain, where many marriages had been annulled on such grounds. Cardinal Pole asked in 1557[38] 'whether they [the clergy] do keep the book or register of christenings, buryings, and marriages, with the names of the godfathers and godmothers'? The register for Banbury (Oxfordshire) illustrates the response to this question (Figure 2). It records the names of godparents throughout 1558. Henrie Bull, for example, was baptised on 24th January 1558; his godparents were Henrie Greene, John Godriche, and Alice Horneslye.

After the accession of Elizabeth, the Church of England did not recognise the crime of spiritual incest. It was therefore not necessary to record the names of godparents. In the Banbury register, their names cease to appear after 21st June 1559. Mention of them did not, however, completely disappear from registers, especially when they were important people:

> 1708, June 28. Charles Grahame, son to Very Rev. Wm D.D. Dean of Wells, by Alice, baptized by Jno Ld Arch Bishop of York. Her Majestie being godmother, and the Dukes of Somerset, Queensberry and Dover, godfathers —born ye 6th' (St. Margaret's, Westminster).

The promises made by godparents were intended to be confirmed by the child when he or she attained sufficient maturity. Unfortunately, the Church of England (unlike the Roman Catholics) did not keep confirmation registers. On very rare occasions, mention might be made of confirmation in the parish register, as in this entry from Tarrant Hinton (Dorset) made in 1809:

> 'Bishop's visitation Sep 1. Elizabeth Frances and Leonora Diggle confirmed'.

National change to the way in which baptismal entries were recorded did not come until the nineteenth century. However, the format proposed by Dade (see above, p. 18) began to be adopted in a few parishes from the late 1770s. For baptisms, Dade registers include the father's name, abode, profession, and descent, together with the mother's name and descent. The names of all four grandparents were to be included, as was the date of birth. In 1782, the Saxton in Elmet register recorded the baptism of:

> 'Ann, 2d dau. of Thomas Prince of Saxton, Lab., son of Richard P. of Thorner, Lab., by Elisabeth his wife, dau of Thomas Haw of Rigton, Lab. [Mother]: Mary, dau of Robert Nicholson of Saxton, taylor, by Alice his wife, dau. of William Webster of Saxton, Lab. [Born] 13 March [Bapt] 13 March'.

---

[38] FRERE, op cit, p.423.

28

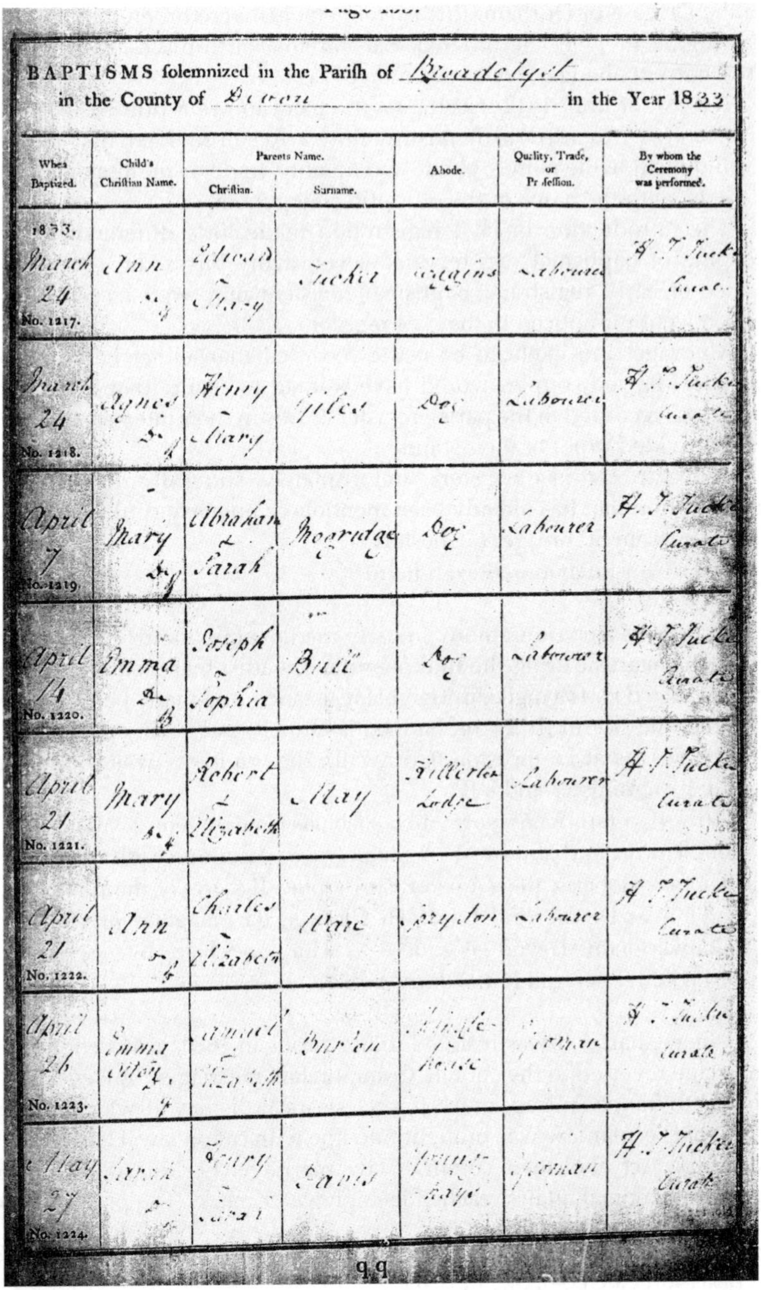

BAPTISMS solemnized in the Parish of _Broadclyst_
in the County of _Devon_ in the Year 18_33_

When Baptized.	Child's Christian Name.	Parents Name.		Abode.	Quality, Trade, or Profession.	By whom the Ceremony was performed.
		Christian.	Surname.			
1833. March 24 No. 1217.	Ann	Edward Mary	Tucker	Huxhams	Labourer	H. T. Tucker Curate
March 24 No. 1218.	Agnes	Henry Mary	Giles	Do.	Labourer	H. T. Tucker Curate
April 7 No. 1219.	Mary	Abraham Sarah	Mogridge	Do.	Labourer	H. T. Tucker Curate
April 14 No. 1220.	Emma	Joseph Sophia	Bull	Do.	Labourer	H. T. Tucker Curate
April 21 No. 1221.	Mary	Robert Elizabeth	May	Killerton Lodge	Labourer	H. T. Tucker Curate
April 21 No. 1222.	Ann	Charles Elizabeth	Ware	Poydon	Labourer	H. T. Tucker Curate
April 26 No. 1223.	Emma Mary	Samuel Elizabeth	Burton	Apple house	Yeoman	H. T. Tucker Curate
May 27 No. 1224.	Sarah	Henry Sarah	Davis	young hayes	Yeoman	H. T. Tucker Curate

q q

Figure 3. Printed baptismal register for Broadclyst, Devon. Devon Record Office, 3594 A-99/PR4.

In the Diocese of Durham, further refinements were ordered by Bishop Barrington in 1796. He ordered that parents' birth-places, rather than their current abodes, should be entered[39].

It was not until 1812 that the requirement to use a printed form for entries was extended to baptisms. Rose's Act provided that entries should include the names, abode and 'quality, trade or profession' of the parents, with the name of the officiating clergyman.

The introduction of civil registration made little difference to the keeping of baptismal registers. However, many births did escape the notice of early registrars. Baptismal registers may well record births which went un-noticed in the civil registers.

Marriages are likely to be better recorded than either baptisms or burials. Married couples would have wanted to ensure that their marriage was recorded in the parish register. It was in their interests to do so, as it provided proof of their status.

Sixteenth century registers, unfortunately, suffer from the heavy abbreviation that has already been mentioned; no entry could be briefer than this from St. Bridget's, Chester:

'Willm Washington wedded 5 Feb 1560'

Marriage was a civil ceremony in early medieval England – and reverted to that status during the Interregnum. The idea that weddings could be conducted by JPs met considerable resistance, and many people either ignored the act of 1653, or had both church and civil ceremonies[40]. Sometimes, as at Launceston (Cornwall), the ceremony was conducted jointly by a minister and a JP:

'1657-8, 5 Jan. Were married by Nicholas Gennis, gent, & Maior of this Towne, and also by Mr. William Oliver, Minister of this Towne, Thomas Roberts, the sonne of Christopher Roberts of the p'ish of Lipton in Devon, and Elizabeth Glanvile the daughter of Oliver Glanvile of this Towne, gent., desesed. Thir banes being by mee published three severall Lords dayes without contradiction'

When Charles II was restored to his throne in 1660, jurisdiction over marriage reverted to the church. Common law marriages, however, continued to be recognised, much to ecclesiastical dismay. It was not until 1753 that secular law was brought into line with canon law. Hardwicke's Marriage Act abolished common law marriage. Ecclesiastical control over matrimonial affairs reached its high water mark. The promoters of

---

[39] BELLINGHAM (2004), op cit, p.57.
[40] DURSTON, CHRISTOPHER. *The family in the English revolution*. Basil Blackwell, 1989, p.75-6.

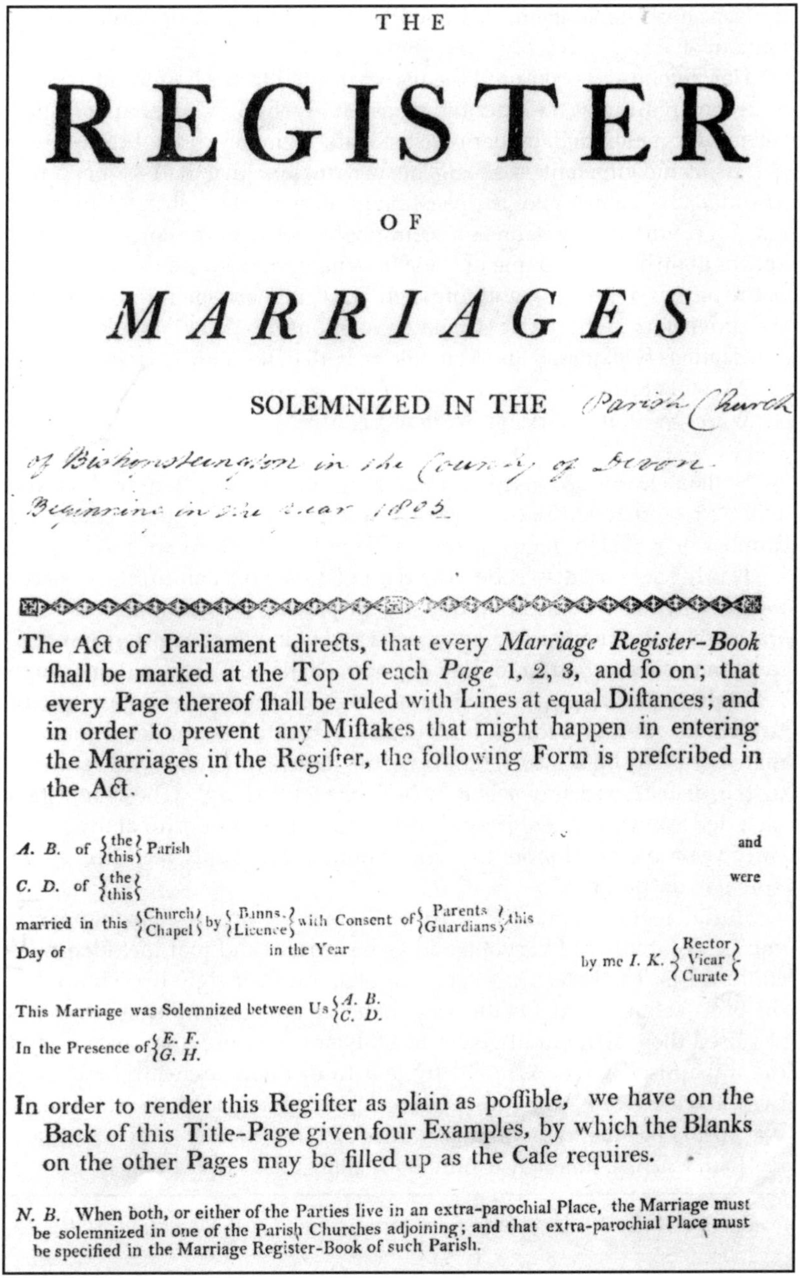

THE
REGISTER

O F

MARRIAGES

SOLEMNIZED IN THE *Parish Church*

of Bishopsteignton in the County of Devon.
Beginning in the Year 1805.

The Act of Parliament directs, that every *Marriage Register-Book* shall be marked at the Top of each *Page* 1, 2, 3, and so on; that every Page thereof shall be ruled with Lines at equal Distances; and in order to prevent any Mistakes that might happen in entering the Marriages in the Register, the following Form is prescribed in the Act.

A. B. of {the}{this} Parish   and

C. D. of {the}{this}   were

married in this {Church}{Chapel} by {Banns.}{Licence} with Consent of {Parents}{Guardians} this

Day of   in the Year   by me I. K. {Rector}{Vicar}{Curate}

This Marriage was Solemnized between Us {A. B.}{C. D.}

In the Presence of {E. F.}{G. H.}

In order to render this Register as plain as possible, we have on the Back of this Title-Page given four Examples, by which the Blanks on the other Pages may be filled up as the Case requires.

N. B. When both, or either of the Parties live in an extra-parochial Place, the Marriage must be solemnized in one of the Parish Churches adjoining; and that extra-parochial Place must be specified in the Marriage Register-Book of such Parish.

Figure 4. Printed title page of the Bishopsteignton, Devon, register, referring to Hardwicke's Act. Devon Record Office 2202A/PR4.

the act would have been dismayed by the reintroduction of civil marriage in 1837.

Hardwicke's Act required the use of printed forms bound into books to record marriages, with effect from 1st April 1754. They give much fuller information than earlier registers, although they did not completely eliminate incompetent scribes. The information that had to be given included the names and parishes of the parties, the date and place of marriage, whether by banns or licence, whether with the consent or parents or guardians, the name of the officiating minister, and the signatures of the parties, witnesses, and minister. The first marriage recorded under the provisions of the act at Huggate (Yorkshire) recorded:

'Thomas Walkington and Mary Sleds, both of this parish, by licence, 2d of February 1755, by John Perry, Curate of Nunburnham. Witnesses: John Clarkson, William Ezart'

William Dade proposed to extend the information required by the 1753 Act to include the occupations, status and ages of both parties. A number of Yorkshire registers after 1779 follow this format[41].

Hardwicke's act also ended the right of most nonconformists to marry in their own churches. Consequently, in parishes where nonconformity was strong, the number of marriages recorded in parish registers jumped.

When civil registration was introduced in 1837, the old marriage registers were closed. The Registrar General supplied each parish with two books of printed forms, both of which had to be completed for each marriage. One book was retained by the parish, the other was returned to the district registrar when it had been filled up[42]. These registers included columns to enter ages and occupations. Unfortunately, in the early years of registration, the age column often simply recorded either 'full age' or 'minor'.

Burial registers provide a fuller record of burials than baptismal entries do of births. Everyone had to be buried, and that included nonconformists. The latter were often insistent on their right to be buried in the parish churchyard. On the other hand, many nonconformist churches acquired their own burial grounds. Only suicides, excommunicates and the unbaptised were excluded by law from the churchyard, and even their burials were sometimes recorded. The registers of St. Anne's, Blackfriars has the following entry for 1579:

'John Hacone, infamously buried for killing himself desperately'

---

[41] BELLINGHAM, ROGER. 'Dade parish registers', *Local population studies* **73**, 2004, p.56.
[42] In places where few events are recorded, the district registrar's copy may not yet have been filled up, and may therefore not yet have been returned to the district registrar.

In 1679, the register of Waterbeach (Cambridgeshire) reads:
'Francis Wilson, excommunicated buried in his orchard'.

Burial registers are basic sources for the history of mortality. They make clear the extent of the impact of plague and other diseases. The register of St. Oswald's, Durham, noted in 1589:
'Sept 20. Robert Maysterman and hys wyffe Margarete Maysterman, of the plage'

Sometimes there were simply too many burials to record. The register of Eaglescliffe (Co.Durham) tells us that (for 1644):-
'in this yeare there died of the plauge in this towne one and twenty people; they are not all buried in the churchyard, and are not in the Register'.

Burial entries can sometimes be very brief, just giving names and dates. A woman might be designated as 'widow' or 'wife of X'. More informative registers might give the names of the parents of young children who died. Sometimes occupations, places of burial, ages, and even officiating clergymen might be specified. After 1769, the register of Falmouth (Cornwall) always gives the age of the deceased. The register of Worcester Cathedral records, on October 16th, 1747:
'Mr.John Field, organist, bur. in the Cloisters, by Mr. Forester'

Occasionally, registers record the payment of a mortuary, that is, an amount due to the priest on the death of one of his parishioners. In 1634, the parson of Ripe (Sussex)
'buried Alice Whitesides Feb 22d who being but one weeke in the parish of Ripe, died as a stranger, for whose mortuary I, John Goffe, had a gowne of Elizabeth her dauther, price 10°'.

Burial in woollen is frequently mentioned, following the Acts of 1666 and 1678 which required burial in a woollen shroud. Affidavits certifying compliance with the law had to be made. Occasionally, a new volume of a burial register begins in 1678. There may also be a separate book for affidavits. Printed forms might also be used. The following entry, from the registers of St. Michael's, Cambridge for 1723, is typical:
'William Brown was buried in woolen'

The idea of burial in woollen offended the sense of decency of some gentry, who preferred the earlier custom of burial in linen. They sometimes regarded the legislation as requiring a tax to be paid, rather than a punishment to be inflicted. When David Walter, esq., the lord of

Godstowe, was buried in Wolvercote (Oxfordshire) in 1679, the interment was:

> 'not according to the Act of Parliament, whereupon an information being given to a justice of the peace, the executor Sir William Walter, ordered 50s to be paid to the poor of the parish, the other 50s being paid to the informer'.

'Chrisom children' frequently appear in burial entries. Strictly speaking, a 'chrisome child' was one who had been baptised, but whose mother had not yet been 'churched'[43]. The term was, however, sometimes used for unbaptised babies. In 1568, the following entry was made in the register of Kirkburton (Yorkshire):

> 'The ix day of December was Jhon March buryd. A Crysm chyld'.

Babies baptised by sixteenth-century midwives because they were not expected to live were often called 'Creature' or 'creatura Christi'. Entries such as this from Staplehurst (Kent) are common:

> '1547. Then was baptized by the Midwyffe, and so buryed, the childe of Thoms Goldham called Creature'.

Changes in the way burial entries were recorded came slowly. Reference has already been made to Dade's proposed format, which began to be adopted in a few parishes in the 1770s. Dade registers include the deceased's name, descent, profession and abode. Dates of both death and burial were to be given, together with the place of burial, the age, and the cause of death. The first such entry in the register of Saxton in Elmet (Yorkshire) was made in 1777:

> 'The Hon[ble] Chaloner Hawke, cornet of the Royal Regiment of British Dragoons, Third son of Edward Lord Hawke of Sunbury by Catherine his wife, dau of Walter Brook of Gateforth, Esq[r]. Died September the 16th and buried in the Chancel in Saxton Church, October 3 [Age] 28. Killed on the road by a Post-chaise"

Rose's Act, 1812, required burial registers to be kept on a printed form in a prescribed way. Henceforth, name, abode, place of burial, age, and the name of the clergymen who presided at the burial service were required. Unfortunately, occupations were not required, nor the names of parents where the deceased was a child.

The introduction of civil registration saw no great change in church burial registers, which continue to be kept. Civil death registers are quite separate. Comparison of the two may be worthwhile.

---

[43] The ceremony of 'churching' was supposed to cleanse mothers before they returned to normal services after giving birth.

| BURIALS in the Parish of _Pyworthy_ in the County of _Devon_ in the Year 18_55_ |||||
Name.	Abode.	When buried.	Age.	By whom the Ceremony was performed.
Mary Ann Staddon _No. 481._	Derril	June 22	2	G. T. Kingdon
Susan Hendron _No. 482._	Marsh	Jan'y 22	52	G. T. Kingdon
John Curtice Oliver _No. 483._	Bounds Cross	June 29	1	G. T. Kingdon
Jane Kellaway _No. 484._	Pyworthy Village	July 10	83	G. T. Kingdon
Rebecca Oliver _No. 485._	Pyworthy	Sept'r 6	81	G. T. Kingdon
Thomas Jones _No. 486._	Pyworthy Village	Sept'r 16	72	G. T. Kingdon
Mary Gloyn _No. 487._	Derril	Oct'r 7	51	G. T. Kingdon
Lewis Luxton _No. 488._	Pyworthy	Nov'r 3	3	G. T. Kingdon

Figure 5. Printed burial register for Pyworthy, Devon. Devon Record Office 2906A/PR8.

7. Original Parish Registers and Copies

Most original parish registers, except those which are still in use, are deposited in local record offices. A summary listing is provided in Cecil Humphery-Smith's *Phillimore atlas and index of parish registers* (3rd ed. Phillimore, 2003). Comprehensive listings of original registers, bishops' transcripts, and other copies, are provided in the county volumes of the *National index of parish registers*, published by the Society of Genealogists.

The volumes of the *National index* do not, however, list registers kept by poor law officers. For workhouse registers, reference must be made to Jeremy Gibson's *Poor law union records* (4 vols. FFHS/Family History Partnership, 1997-2008).

A handful of other non-parochial registers are held by the National Archives. Mention has already been made of the Fleet registers. Registers from Greenwich Hospital, the Foundling Hospital, Chelsea Royal Hospital, and a number of similar institutions are also held. Some of these are available on 'BMD Registers' **www.bmdregisters.co.uk**.

Non-parochial registers also include overseas registers, and registers of events at sea. For these, reference should be made to:
* *The British Overseas: a guide to records of their births, baptisms, marriages, deaths, and burials available in the United Kingdom*. 3rd ed. Guildhall Library, 1994.
* WATTS, CHRISTOPHER T., & WATTS, MICHAEL J. *Tracing births deaths and marriages at sea*. Society of Genealogists Enterprises, 2004.
* Births Marriages and Deaths Overseas
  www.history.ac.uk/gh.overseas.htm

Many record offices have published listings of the registers they hold. Occasionally, lists of local parish registers will be found on the websites of family history societies. *Genuki* **www.genuki.org.uk** provides a great deal of information on original registers, transcripts, and indexes.

A number of record offices are able to supply microform copies of original parish registers in their possession. These are not always easy to read, especially if the original has faded or suffered other damage.

Many parish registers have been transcribed and published. Even in 1910, Cox was able to publish a ten page listing of published registers[44].

---

[44] Cox, op cit, p.272-82.

More up to date listings can be found in the county volumes of Raymond's *British genealogical library guides* (formerly *British genealogical bibliographies*) series. Published registers can be found in libraries worldwide (and not just in the relevant counties). There are, for example, good collections of parish registers from all over England in Bristol Public Library, and in the State Library of Victoria, Melbourne.

Societies and others have published many series of parish registers. Over 1400 marriage registers are transcribed in *Phillimore's parish registers* series. The Parish Register Society published over 100 registers from many counties in the late nineteenth and early twentieth centuries. 89 registers (mainly for London) were published by the Harleian Society. Bedfordshire is the only county for which all pre-1812 parish registers have been published; this was the work of Bedfordshire County Council **www.bedfordshire.gov.uk** (search Bedfordshire Parish Register series). There have been societies devoted to the publication of parish registers in a number of counties; those for Lancashire, Shropshire, Staffordshire, and Yorkshire have been particularly prolific. Societies have also existed in Buckinghamshire, Northumberland & Durham, and Surrey. The Parish Register Transcription Society **www.prtsoc.org.uk** has recently commenced publishing registers for Hampshire, Norfolk, West Sussex, and elsewhere. County record societies have also published registers. For example, both the Devon and Cornwall Record Society, and the Cumberland and Westmorland Antiquarian & Archaeological Society, have issued many registers for their areas.

A number of individuals have also been prolific publishers of parish registers. Sir Thomas Phillipps printed a few in the early nineteenth century. F.A. Crisp edited numerous registers from East Anglia. F.H.A.Hervey included a number of registers in his series of *Suffolk green books*. More recently, Robert Cottrell's *Thames & Medway Riverside series* **hometown.aol.com/rjcindex/trueflare.html** includes many registers from the London area, on fiche or CD.

Many transcripts and extracts from parish registers were published in genealogical journals of the late nineteenth and early twentieth centuries, such as *Miscellanea genealogica et heraldica* (1868-1938) and the *Genealogist* (1877-1921). These are listed in Stuart Raymond's *British genealogical periodicals: a bibliography of their contents* (FFHS, 3 vols in 5, 1991-3). Similar material is also frequently found in the transactions of county historical and archaeological societies, and in journals such as *Gloucestershire notes and queries*.

In the last three decades, many family history societies have transcribed, indexed, and published registers, sometimes on microfiche or CD. The publications of Kent Family History Society, and of the Birmingham & Midland Society for Genealogy and Heraldry, are particularly noteworthy. These publications are usually listed on society websites (listed at **www.genuki.org.uk/Societies**). Comprehensive listings, although now rather out of date, are provided by Elizabeth Hampson's *Current publications from member societies* (10th ed. 1999), and John Perkins, *Current publications on microfiche by member societies* (5th ed. 2002). A comprehensive collection of published registers is held by the Society of Genealogists, whose library catalogue **www.sog.org.uk** (click 'Sogcat') provides the most up to date listing. Another major collection is held by the British Library, whose catalogue is online at **catalogue.bl.uk**.

There are also a huge number of parish register transcripts and indexes on the internet[45]. It takes two volumes to list them all. Stuart Raymond's *Births marriages and deaths on the web* (2nd ed. 2 vols., 2005) provides a comprehensive listing, which will be regularly updated. Many web pages offer digitised images of published registers, especially from the Phillimore series. The 'Cheshire Parish Register Project' **www.csc.liv.ac.uk/~cprdb** is currently preparing computerised transcripts of registers for the whole county.

Surprisingly – and disappointingly – few original registers have been digitised. A handful can be found on the Welsh 'Gathering the Jewels' site **www.gtj.org.uk** (search for 'parish register'). London Metropolitan Archives is planning a digitisation programme. But the only important collection currently available is that provided by Medway Archives **cityark.medway.gov.uk** (click 'parish registers online'). Hopefully, more record offices will follow their example.

There are many unpublished transcripts and indexes of parish registers. It has been common practice to make three copies of these documents, one for the local studies library or record office, one for the local family history society, and one for the Society of Genealogists. Those held by the Society can be identified on its online library catalogue **www.sog.org.uk**.

---

[45] Most *National index of parish registers* volumes pre-date the internet, and therefore do not mention these.

8. *Associated Documents*

A. Bishops' Transcripts

Annual returns of parish register entries began to be made to diocesan bishops (or, occasionally, other ecclesiastical officials), from the beginning of Queen Elizabeth I's reign. In the Diocese of Canterbury, for example, bishops' transcripts (BTs) survive from 1561, as they do in the Archdeaconry of Lincoln. The requirement for these returns was enshrined in canon law in 1598, and again in 1604. The 1604 canon made it clear that returns should end on 25th March each year.

In most dioceses, BTs survive from the adoption of these canons until at least 1837. They become increasingly rare in the late nineteenth century. The most recent BT known to exist is dated 1932, and is for Over Tabley, Cheshire.

Survival of BTs has been patchy. None were made during the Interregnum, 1649-1660. In Canterbury diocese, two sets of transcripts were made, one for the Archdeacon, one for the Bishop's Consistory Court. By contrast, there are none at all for most of Essex prior to 1800. The Registrar of the Diocese of London certified in 1800 that 'it is not the custom within the Diocese of London for any return to be made to the Bishop's Registry of either burials or baptisms[46]. Many peculiars did not send in BTs, until Rose's Act 1812 made it a legal requirement for them to do so. Jeremy Gibson's *Bishops' transcripts and marriage licences ...* (4th ed. FFHS, 1997) provides a nation-wide listing of what is available. The county volumes of the *National index of parish registers* provide detailed listings for each parish.

If BTs are available, they should always be compared with parish registers. Some are identical, some provide abbreviated entries, leaving out detail, some provide more details than are recorded in the register. Occasionally, BTs may provide more entries than are found in the register. For example, 18 marriages are recorded in the 1687 BT for St.Nicholas, Gloucester, but not in the parish register. It may be that some clergy thought BTs were more important than the register itself; after all, the latter was rarely consulted, whereas the BTs could be read by their superiors.

---

[46] Burn, op cit, p.201.

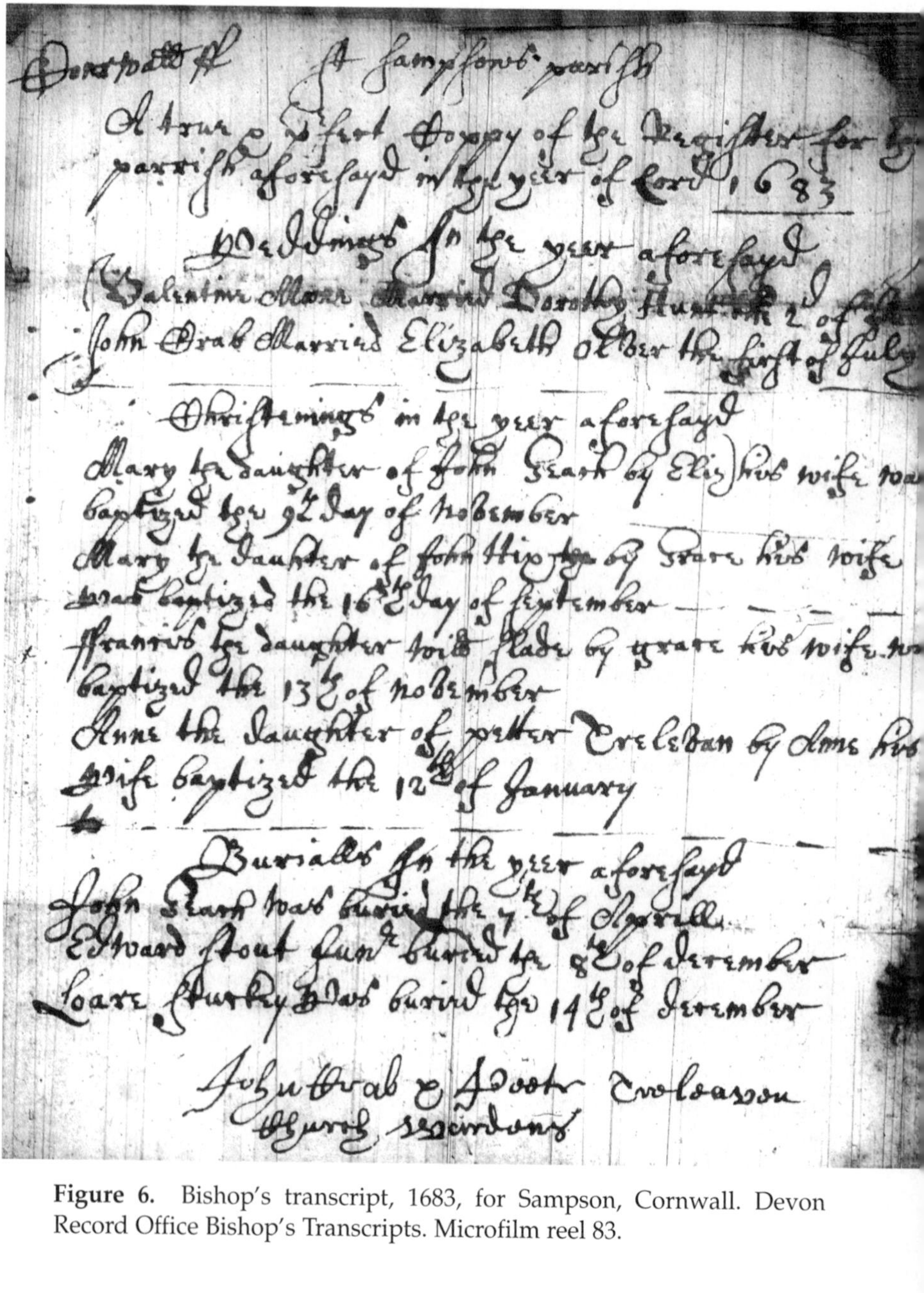
Cornwall ss St Sampsons parish
A true & perfect Coppy of the Register for the
parish aforesayd in the year of Lord 1683
Weddings in the year aforesayd
Valentine More married Dorothy Hunt the 2d of ...
John Crab Married Elizabeth Olver the first of July
Christenings in the year aforesayd
Mary the daughter of John Searle by Eliz his wife was
baptized the 9th day of November
Mary the daughter of John Hix by Grace his wife
was baptized the 16th day of September
ffrances the daughter of Wm Slade by Grace his wife was
baptized the 13th of November
Anne the daughter of Peter Treleavan by Anne his
wife baptized the 12th of January
Burialls in the year aforesayd
John Searle was buried the 7th of Aprill
Edward Stout Jun buried the 8th of December
Loare Sturtey was buried the 14th of December
John Crab & Peeter Treleavan
Church wardens

Figure 6. Bishop's transcript, 1683, for Sampson, Cornwall. Devon Record Office Bishop's Transcripts. Microfilm reel 83.

B. Banns Registers

According to canon law, the marriage ceremony had to be preceded by the proclamation of the intention to marry, unless a licence was obtained. The calling of these 'banns' before marriage was required by a Lateran Council decree of 1215. The canons of 1575 required that the public had to be 'openly asked' if they knew of any impediment to a marriage 'on three several Sundays or holidays in the service time'[47]. Banns continue to be called even today.

Until the eighteenth century, registers rarely mention the calling of banns. The main exception to this rule took place during the Interregnum, when many registers were compiled by lay 'parish registers'. They sometimes recorded the 'publication' of marriages, that is, the calling of banns, as in this example from Aldenham (Hertfordshire):

'A contracte of matrymony betwene John Towers and Elizabeth Edwardes both of this parish, Published on March the 27 and April the 3 and 10; But broke of and never maryed'

Hardwicke's Act, 1753, required registers of banns to be kept. Sometimes the printed marriage registers made provision for banns to be entered on the same page as marriages, sometimes they were entered in the first half of the book, and marriages in the second. Alternatively, there might be an entirely separate banns register.

In some parishes, new banns registers were commenced when the Marriage Act 1824 required that banns should be read directly from the register, rather than from scraps of paper. From 1837, banns registers had to be kept separately from marriage registers. At Tarrant Hinton (Dorset) a separate register of 'banns of marriage of those not married here' was kept. In 1766, it records:

'William Caish of this parish and Joan Webb of Sherborn parish, March 16, 23 and April 6'.

For some reason, this entry was signed by the rector of Gunville, and the vicar of Monkton, as well as the rector of Tarrant Hinton.

Banns registers have not been treated well. Many have been lost. Nevertheless, it is worth checking whether they do survive, as they may add detail to what is already known, and provide clues to further research. If the parties to an intended marriage came from different parishes, then their banns should be recorded in two different banns registers. Comparison of the two with the marriage register may provide additional detail, such as places of abode.

Associated with the banns register are the written notifications which each spouse was supposed to submit when requesting the calling of

---

[47] Bray, op cit, p.215.

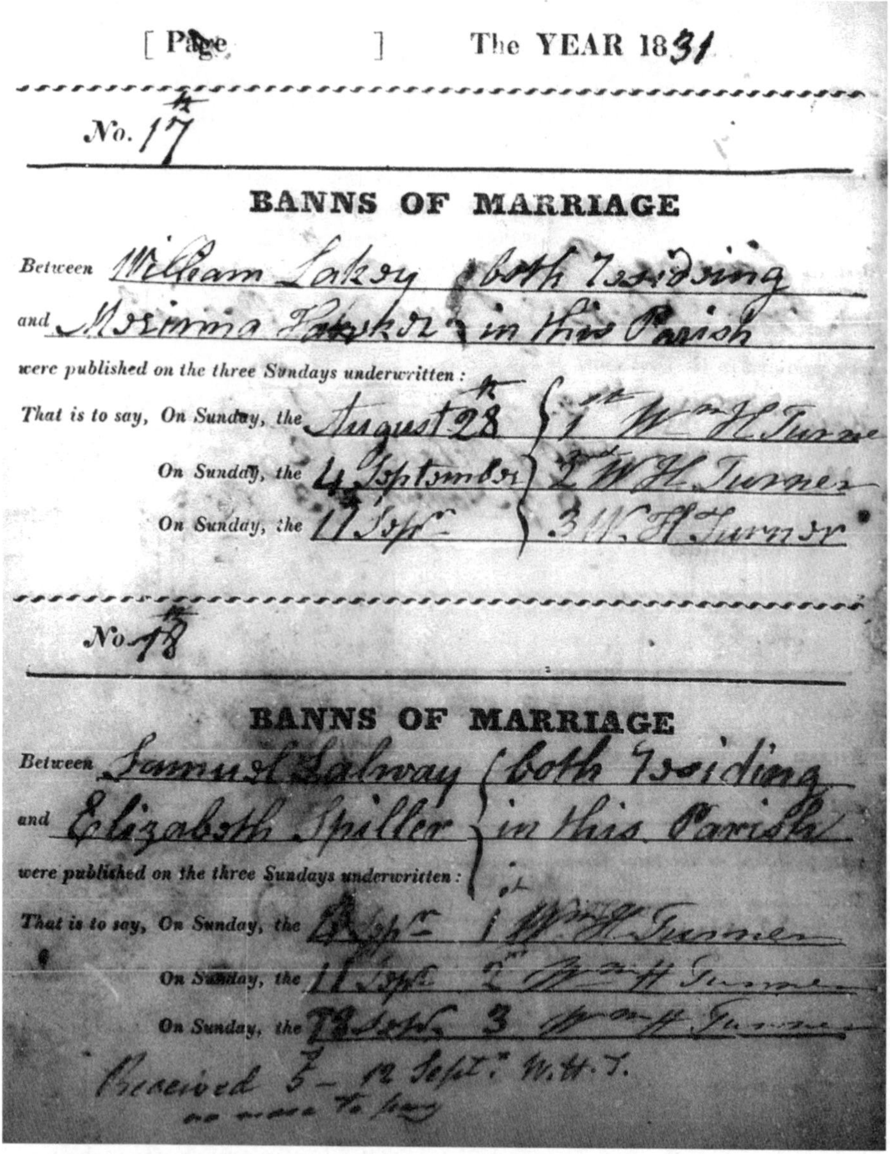

[Page] The YEAR 1831

No. 17

BANNS OF MARRIAGE

Between William Lakey (both residing
and Morinna Parker in this Parish
were published on the three Sundays underwritten:
That is to say, On Sunday, the August 28 { 1st Wm H Turner
On Sunday, the 4 September } 2nd W H Turner
On Sunday, the 11 Sepr } 3 W H Turner

No. 18

BANNS OF MARRIAGE

Between Samuel Salway (both residing
and Elizabeth Spiller in this Parish
were published on the three Sundays underwritten:
That is to say, On Sunday, the 4 Sepr 1st Wm H Turner
On Sunday, the 11 Sepr 2nd Wm H Turner
On Sunday, the 18 Sepr 3 Wm H Turner

Received 5/- 12 Septr W.H.T.
no more to pay

Figure 7. Banns register for Dalwood, Devon, 1831. Devon Record Office, 324Z.

banns. Very occasionally these survive amongst parish records, and may provide additional information. The Marriage Act 1822 required affidavits containing detailed information on both spouses to be submitted, with effect from 1st September 1822. Unfortunately for genealogists, this requirement was repealed as from March 1823. Affidavits for this brief period do occasionally survive[48].

Banns registers do not prove that a marriage took place, merely that one was intended. The entry from Aldenham quoted above relates to a marriage that clearly did not take place. Registers are seldom so explicit. Banns may provide valuable information, regardless of whether a marriage took place. On very rare occasions the banns register might record an objection. But an entry in a marriage register is normally required to prove the fact of marriage.

C. Marriage Licence Allegations and Bonds

It was possible to circumvent the need for banns to be called by obtaining a marriage licence. Such licences had been granted in the medieval period, but became much more common after the Reformation. Sixteenth-century licences in Exeter Diocese only gave exemption from one or two callings of banns, or allowed marriages to take place in a season when they would otherwise be forbidden, such as Lent. Later licences granted permission to marry 'without the publication or proclamation of the banns of matrimony and at any time in the year'.

A licence enabled a marriage to take place quickly, and could be necessary if a couple were away from home. Between 1754 and 1837, nonconformists often preferred to marry by licence rather than by banns: they wanted as little to do with the church as possible. Marriage licences also became a status symbol. The gentry thought it was vulgar to have banns called in church.

Licences to marry were granted by bishops and their surrogates. They could also be granted by some archdeacons, and by those who held jurisdiction in peculiar parishes. The archbishops had the power to grant special licences, which enabled the recipients to marry in any church. Canon law required most couples to marry in a parish where one of them resided, and common licences should have contained this restriction. This aspect of the law, however, was frequently flouted.

The marriage licence was normally given to the couple, who presented it to the minister officiating. Most licences have been lost. However, two other documents may survive. In some dioceses, registers of licences

---

[48] '1822-23: the *annus mirabilis* of genealogy', *Genealogists magazine* **21**(3), 1983, p.88-9.

issued were kept. Exeter diocese has registers with contemporary indexes. In November 1777, for example, a licence was granted

'to John Wright of Hatherleigh, yeoman, and Sarah Partridge of Washford Pyne, spinster'.

Application for a licence was made by submitting an allegation, a sworn statement that there was no impediment to the marriage. These allegations were retained, and usually give names, ages (which should be treated with caution), places of abode, and occupations/status of both spouses. If a minor was involved, the name of a consenting parent should also be given.

From 1579 until 1823, the authorities also required a marriage bond to be entered into by two bondsmen. These were intended to give security to the issuers if the conditions of the bond were not met. The conditions were that there was no impediment to the marriage, and that any necessary parental consent had been given. The canons of 1604 imposed a further condition - that the marriage take place in a parish where one of the parties lived[49]. If these conditions were not met, the bondsmen (who generally included the groom) stood to lose the amount specified in the bond. Until 1733, the first part of a bond was in Latin. Bonds generally give the names of the parties and bondsmen, perhaps their residences and occupations (or status), and the date. The name of the second bondsman was often fictitious; in Surrey, for example, after 1770 his name was always John Doe. Sometimes bonds for minors were annotated by a parent, indicating that permission had been granted.

The Marriage Act 1822, which required an affidavit to be sworn when banns were to be called[50], also required an affidavit when a licence was requested. This was repealed in 1823, but for seven months, from September 1st 1822 to March 31st 1823, every applicant for a marriage licence had to make an affidavit stating the ages and marital status of both parties. If one was a minor, then the written and witnessed consent of a parent had to be given. Ages were proved by presenting baptismal certificates[51].

Marriage bonds and allegations survive in diocesan record offices (which are usually county record offices). Most have been indexed; many have been printed. It is worth checking for both a bond and an allegation, since the information in them may differ. Full details of surviving records, and of indexes to them, are given in Jeremy Gibson's *Bishops transcripts and marriage licences, bonds and allegations* (5th ed. FFHS, 2001). Unfortunately, some of the older published editions are not always accu-

---

[49] Bray, op cit, p.403.
[50] See above, p.43.
[51] Discussed below, p.46.

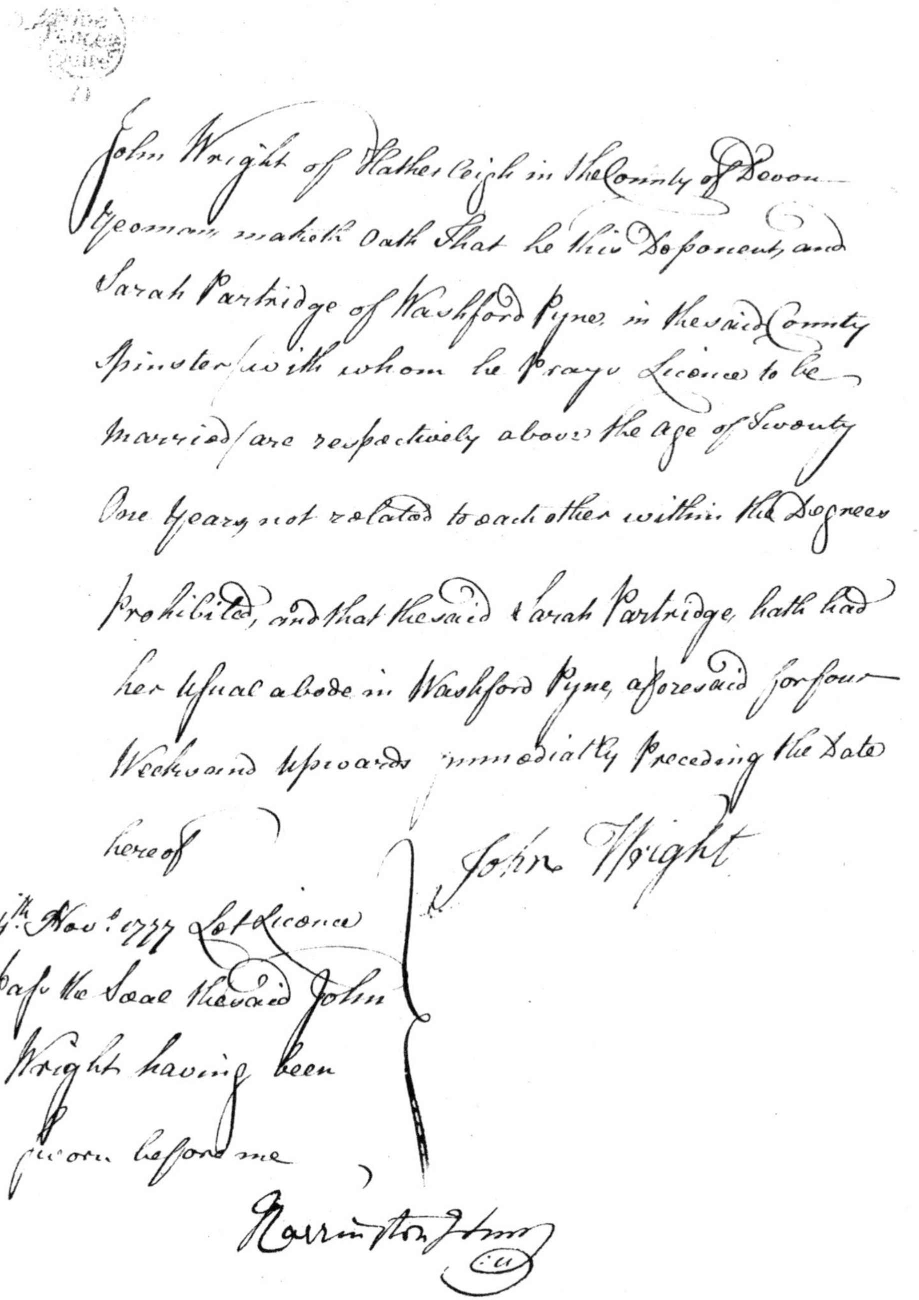

John Wright of Hatherleigh in the County of Devon Yeoman maketh Oath That he this Deponent, and Sarah Partridge of Washford Pyne, in the said County Spinster/with whom he prays Licence to be married/are respectively above the age of Twenty One Years, not related to each other within the Degrees Prohibited, and that the said Sarah Partridge, hath had her Usual abode in Washford Pyne, aforesaid for four Weeks and upwards immediatly Preceding the Date hereof

John Wright

4th Nov. 1777 Let Licence pass the Seal the said John Wright having been sworn before me

Harrington John

Figure 8. Marriage allegation of John Wright of Hatherleigh. Devon Record Office Marriage allegations box 71.

rate, and do not necessarily give full details. They should always, if possible, be checked against originals.

The warning that was given above concerning banns registers also applies to marriage licence records: they do not prove that the marriage actually took place. If a marriage licence bond or allegation is discovered, and proof that the marriage took place is required, search for an entry in a marriage register. Licences were valid for three months, so searches can be limited to that period.

D. Baptismal Certificates

Certificates of baptism are rarely mentioned in genealogical textbooks. No record of their issue seems to have been kept, but many can be found amongst personal memoranda, and in official records. Their importance in 1822-3 has already been mentioned.

As the eighteenth and nineteenth centuries progressed, an increasing number of people needed to prove their ages, especially if they wished to serve in the armed forces or the civil service. Before the introduction of civil registration, proof was often provided by baptismal certificates, which could be obtained from incumbents. Many baptismal certificates for army officers may be found amongst the National Archives War Office records. For the period 1777-1868, they can be found in WO32/8903-20, for 1755-1908 in WO42. Royal Naval officers' passing certificates, found in ADM6, ADM13, and ADM107, often have baptism certificates attached[52]. The Society of Genealogists now holds Civil Service evidences of age, which include many baptism certificates dating from 1752 to 1948. They are indexed at 'Find My Past' **www.findmypast.com**.

---

[52] For more details, see the guides to these classes on the National Archives website **www.nationalarchives.gov.uk** (click on 'Research' and 'Research Guides').

9. Indexes to Parish Registers

Innumerable indexes to parish registers are now available; some have already been referred to briefly. Marriage indexes are listed in Jeremy Gibson, et al, *Marriage indexes for family historians* (9th ed. Family History Partnership, 2008). Some baptism and burial indexes are listed in his *Specialist indexes for family historians* (3rd ed. Family History Partnership, forthcoming).

The *International Genealogical Index*, usually referred to as the *IGI*, is the most comprehensive index available. It covers baptisms and marriages, but not burials. In addition to parish registers, it also indexes many nonconformist and Roman Catholic registers. Entries are continually being added - although the index is still far from giving complete coverage. The *IGI* indexes the microform collection of birth, marriage and death registers held by the Family History Library in Salt Lake City. This library is run by the Church of Jesus Christ of Latter Day Saints, referred to below as the LDS, and popularly known as the Mormons. It holds the largest collection of birth, marriage and death registers in the world; coverage is world-wide, and includes a substantial percentage of English parish registers. The index is available on the 'Family Search' website **www.familysearch.org**. Many libraries hold a microfiche version. The fiche was issued in 1992, so may now be outdated. A CD version is also available; this is known as the *British vital records index* (2nd ed. 2002) and can be purchased via 'Family Search'. The website provides more information than either the microfiche or the CD, and is also more up to date.

There are two sources for entries in the *IGI*. 'Extracted records' are indexes of registers of baptisms (or sometimes births) and marriages. These may be parish registers, bishops' transcripts, or nonconformist registers. 'Submitted records' have been submitted by researchers tracing their own families. Extracted records are generally much more reliable than submitted records. The latter may be based on no more than speculation.

It is important to appreciate that the *IGI* is only an index. It is not the original record. The index records the name of the individual, the type of event, the date, the place, names of parents (sometimes), and the Family History Library microfilm number. Much more information than this may be given in the actual registers. For example, from 1754, marriage registers include the signatures of bride and groom, and also of witnesses. From 1813, baptism registers include the father's address and occupation. None of this information is given in the index.

The *IGI* is based on documents that have been filmed by the LDS. Those documents are not necessarily original registers. They may be printed, typescript, or handwritten copies. Bishops' transcripts have also been filmed. Researchers need to know what it is that they are looking at. The accuracy of any copy should always be checked against the original register if possible.

Registers that have been filmed and indexed are listed on Hugh Wallis's 'IGI Batch Numbers' site **freepages.genealogy.rootsweb. ancestry.com/~hughwallis/IGIBatchNumbers.htm**. Many of the parish pages on 'Genuki' **www.genuki.org.uk** provide film numbers of local registers that have been copied. Films can be borrowed for a small fee through any of the LDS worldwide network of Family History Centres. These are listed on 'Family Search' **www.familysearch.org**. Alternatively, the *IGI* could be checked directly against original registers, or with printed or digitised copies.

The *IGI* only includes baptisms and marriages. It does not include burials. In order to fill this gap, the member societies of the Federation of Family History Societies are compiling the *National Burial Index*. The *NBI* is an index of parish registers and bishops transcripts, although the indexers may have used copies of these documents rather than the originals. Coverage depends on the willingness of family history societies to participate. Many societies have concentrated on the period from 1813, when burial registers began to be compiled using printed forms. Each entry gives the name, the date of burial, the place, the age (if recorded), and the name of the society or the individual who made the entry.

Like the *IGI*, the *NBI* is just an index, a finding aid. More information is likely to be found in the original source. The society responsible for making a particular entry may be willing to check that source.

The second CD edition of the *NBI* was published by the FFHS in 2004, and includes 13,000,000+ entries. Work is continuing, and further updates are planned. Some county portions of the index can be searched on the internet, at 'Family History Online' **www.familyhistoryonline.org.uk**, and at 'Find My Past' **www.findmypast.co.uk**, on a pay per view basis. 'Find My Past' is planning to supplement its online index with full transcripts of burial registers, and perhaps of monumental inscriptions, where these are available. It should be noted that monumental inscriptions are not indexed in the *NBI*.

A wide variety of other indexes are also available. *Boyd's Marriage Index* is probably the largest. It was compiled between 1925 and 1955. Copies of the original typescript are held by the Society of Genealogists, the College of Arms, and the Family History Library in Salt Lake City.

County portions of the original index were also made available to a number of local repositories. A detailed guide to the typescript is provided by Steel[53]. The 6th edition of *A list of parishes in Boyd's marriage index* was published by the Society of Genealogists in 1994. The entire index is now available online at 'British Origins' **www.britishorigins.com**, on a pay per view basis.

Parish registers, bishops' transcripts, marriage licences, and a few banns registers were indexed by Boyd, although it is probable that many of his entries are based on copies, rather than on original registers. He and his team indexed some 7,000,000 names in 4300 registers – perhaps 15% of all English marriages between 1538 and 1837. The index covers every English county, and is particularly strong for East Anglia (including 12,000 entries from Suffolk marriage licence allegations).

The same site also has the 'London burials index 1538-1872'. This index combines 240,000 entries from 'Boyd's London burials', with 35,000 entries from Cliff Webb's 'London City Burials'.

Another important index is currently in the possession of the Institute of Heraldic & Genealogical Studies, in Canterbury **www.ihgs.org.uk**. This is Pallot's index, which includes baptisms and marriages, and was originally compiled for commercial purposes. Indexing commenced as long ago as 1813. A handful of the registers indexed have since been lost, so the index may be the only surviving source for some information. Conversely, much of the index was destroyed during the Second World War. What remains has been digitised, and is now available online at **www.ancestry.co.uk**, by subscription. It is also available on two CDs, *Pallot's marriage index 1780-1837*, and *Pallot's baptism index, 1780-1837*.

The marriage portion of Pallot's index includes entries from 2,500 parishes in 38 counties, plus entries from all but two of the parishes in the old City of London, and from a few Welsh parishes. There are a total of 1,695,352 entries, covering the period 1780 to 1837. Not all parishes are indexed for the whole period; for many, the indexing only covers 1790 to 1812.

Pallot's baptism index suffered more severely during the war. It once had 12,000,000 entries, but only 201,976 now survive. Registers from 22 London parishes, 27 parishes in other counties, and a few Welsh parishes, are indexed.

An index of more recent provenance is provided by the Joiner Marriage Index **www.joinermarriageindex.com**, which offers a pay per view service. Its focus is primarily on Northern England, although it extends as far south as Hertfordshire. The website has over 1,000,000 entries; another 600,000 are available off-line.

---

[53] STEEL, op cit, p.201-5.

There are numerous indexes covering particular counties and small-er areas. Reference has already been made to the burial indexes available on Family History Online **www.familyhistoryonline.org.uk**. This site also hosts many baptism and marriage indexes, plus a few indexes to banns registers

10. *The Uses of Parish Registers*

Parish registers have many uses to the present-day historian. They are obviously key sources for the family historian seeking proof of the descent of ancestors, indeed, they are one of the few sources which were designed for the use of genealogists. They are also vital sources for the local historian. The history of English demography is largely based upon them[54]. The techniques of aggregative analysis and family reconstitution have been applied to hundreds of registers, and have enabled historians to study topics such as the periodicity of marriage, servants in husbandry, and the incidence of bastardy. The history of the family, literacy, and occupations, are all readily studied using parish register data. Many demographic studies based on parish registers have been published in *Local population studies*[55].

Both family and local historians need to be aware of the pitfalls of using parish registers. They should be particularly careful when using indexes and transcripts, including those in printed books and on the internet. These are useful, sometimes very useful. But they do leave plenty of room for human error to creep in.

The accuracy of transcripts and indexes always needs to be checked. Some transcripts are very accurate. Others are woeful. Surnames are easily mis-read. Entries which are out of sequence are easily missed altogether. Entries may be abbreviated, with important information omitted. Illegible entries may be passed by without notice. BTs are not necessarily collated with the original register. There may be gaps in the register, or in the BTs. Names of witnesses may not be copied. There are many possibilities for error[56]. It is important to assess the value of the evidence provided by both indexes and transcripts, by comparing them with the original registers.

---

[54] England's demographic history is summarised in HINDE, ANDREW. *England's population: a history since the Domesday study.* Hodder Arnold, 2003. This book also includes up to date discussions of 'sources and methods' for studying English population.

[55] A selection of these are printed in DRAKE, M., ed. *Population studies from parish registers: a selection of readings from Local population studies.* 1982.

[56] STEEL, op cit, p.191-200 offers a detailed discussion of errors in copying and indexing.

The fact that information is not given in a transcript or index does not mean that it is not in the original register. The fact that information is given in a transcript or index does not mean that it is accurate. An index in particular should not be treated as a transcript; the original register may give much more information.

Transcribers and indexers have not always been expert palaeographers, nor have they necessarily followed consistent procedures in their tasks. Indeed, statements of editorial methodology are infrequent in published registers. Ideally, a published register should be a letter by letter, word by word, exact copy of the original. Practicality, however, dictates that some form of summarising must take place. Such words as 'was baptised' or 'sepultus erat' do not need constant repetition. Steel has set out some 'recommendations for copying and indexing parish registers'[57]. His proposals ought to be considered by every transcriber, although they do need modification if the transcript is intended for a web page. It is questionable, incidentally, whether small parish registers transcribed for the web need indexes. Where all the entries are included on one page, the 'search' function on web browsers performs the same function as an index. Every transcript ought to have a statement of the methodology used by the editor. The reader does need to know what relationship a transcription bears to the original text.

It is also important to assess the accuracy and comprehensiveness of original registers[58]. Are there gaps in the chronology? Did scribes record every event that they should have done? And is the information they recorded correct?

Accuracy can be checked by comparing registers with bishops' transcripts, or with marriage licence allegations/bonds. Sometimes, these sources may give additional information. Differences between the registers and bishops transcripts may be significant, in view of the fact that the latter are supposed to be transcripts of the former. Other sources, such as wills, manorial rolls, poor law records, etc., may also be examined and compared with the evidence of parish registers.

Comprehensiveness must also be checked. Parish registers were supposed to include all vital events in their area. There are various reasons why they increasingly fell short of achieving this aim.

The extent of non-registration of baptisms gradually increased in the eighteenth century, especially towards its end. In 1700, most babies were baptised within a week or so of birth. By 1800, perhaps 30% escaped

---

[57] STEEL, op cit, p.207-16.

[58] For the following paragraphs, see EVERSLEY, D.E.C., LASLETT, PETER, & WRIGLEY, E.A. *An introduction to English historical demography from the sixteenth to the nineteenth century.* Weidenfield and Nicolson, 1966; and HINDE, op cit, p.163-73.

registration[59]. The fact that the gap between birth and baptism had widened considerably may have been one cause of under-registration.

Nonconformists (except, in the early days, Methodists) generally baptised their own babies. Quakers and Baptists did not baptise babies at all. In strong nonconformist areas, under-registration is therefore likely to be higher than elsewhere.

In cities, the sheer numbers of babies to baptise, weddings to celebrate, and burials to conduct, overwhelmed the parish clergy. Their record keeping suffered accordingly, resulting in under-registration. Also, many people did not bother to have their babies baptised.

Nevertheless, most people continued to be married in the Church of England. There were 122,496 marriages in 1841, according to the Registrar General[60]. Of these, 114,371 took place in the established church, and only 5882 in other places of worship.

The comprehensiveness of parish registers can be tested by comparing them with listings of inhabitants. Tax lists, militia rolls, the 1641/2 Protestation, and the Compton Census of 1676, all provide evidence that can be used in assessing the size of a parish's population. By using multipliers that take account of people who were not counted in these sources (such as women and children), it is possible to arrive at rough estimates of the total populations of particular parishes. Such estimates can then be compared with the numbers of recorded baptisms and burials. There would normally be at least 20 births for every 1,000 inhabitants. If it can be shown that a particular register records fewer baptisms than this, then its plausibility must be questioned.

Parish registers have suffered many vicissitudes over the centuries. Few registers survive from 1538. Of those that do, most are transcripts made after 1598. Cliff Webb[61] has calculated that the average English register commences in 1611. London has the best record of survival; there, the average starting date is 1578, despite the Great Fire of 1666.

Many parishes do not have all the registers which they ought to have. The Spaniards destroyed the registers of Paul (Cornwall) when they raided the coast in 1595. Parliamentary soldiers tore leaves out of the register of Wimpole (Cambridgeshire). The register of Cottenham (Cambridgeshire) was destroyed by fire in 1676. Many others have been lost through neglect, damp, and infestation. We are very fortunate that so many do survive.

---

[59] DRAKE, MICHAEL, & FINNEGAN, RUTH. *Sources and methods for family and community historians: a handbook.* 2nd ed. Cambridge University Press, 1997, p.72-3.

[60] EVERSLEY, op cit, p.51-2.

[61] WEBB, CLIFF. 'The starting dates of English and Welsh parish registers', *Genealogists' magazine* **24**(2), 1992, p.59-61.

Further Reading

The classic text on parish registers is:

STEEL, D.J. *National index of parish registers. Volume 1. Sources of births, marriages and deaths before 1837 (1).* Society of Genealogists, 1968.

A number of older texts are also useful:

BURN, JOHN SOUTHERDEN. *Parish registers in England.* 2nd ed. John Russell Smith, 1862.

COX, J.CHARLES. *The parish registers of England.* Methuen, 1910. (reprinted EP Publishing, 1974)

WATERS, R.E. CHESTER. *Parish registers in England.* Longmans, Green & Co., 1887. (reprinted Family History Society of Cheshire, 1999).

Local historians and demographers will need to consult:

EVERSLEY, D.E.C., LASLETT, PETER, & WRIGLEY, E.A. *An introduction to English historical demography from the sixteenth to the nineteenth century.* Weidenfield and Nicolson, 1966.

HINDE, ANDREW. *England's population: a history since the Domesday survey.* Hodder Arnold, 2003,

TATE, W.E. *The parish chest: a study in the records of parochial administration in England.* 3rd ed. Phillimore, 1983.

The fullest listings of original registers and copies are supplied by the county volumes of the *National Index of parish registers.* Parish registers transcribed and indexed on the internet are listed in:

RAYMOND, STUART A. *Births marriages and deaths on the web.* 2nd ed. 2 vols. FFHS, 2005.

Many indexes are listed in:

GIBSON, JEREMY, HAMPSON, ELIZABETH, & RAYMOND, STUART. *Marriage indexes for family historians.* Family History Partnership, 2008.

For the location of bishops' transcripts and marriage licence records, see:

GIBSON, JEREMY. *Bishops' transcripts and marriage licences, bonds and allegations: a guide to their location and indexes.* 4th ed. FFHS, 1997.

Place Name Index

Personal Name Index

Subject Index

Also available from the Family History Partnership

NETTING YOUR ANCESTORS

Tracing Family History on the Internet

Stuart A. Raymond

www.thefamilyhistorypartnership.co.uk